UKULELE

100 Most Beautiful
CHRISTMAS SONGS

T0088546

ISBN 978-1-5400-5556-9

Visit Hal Leonard Online at
www.halleonard.com

Contact us:
Hal Leonard
7777 West Bluemound Road
Milwaukee, WI 53213
Email: info@halleonard.com

In Europe, contact:
Hal Leonard Europe Limited
42 Wigmore Street
Marylebone, London, W1U 2RN
Email: info@halleonardeurope.com

In Australia, contact:
Hal Leonard Australia Pty. Ltd.
4 Lentara Court
Cheltenham, Victoria, 3192 Australia
Email: info@halleonard.com.au

Contents

All Is Well

Words and Music by Michael W. Smith and Wayne Kirkpatrick

First note

Verse
Gently

1. All is well, all is well. An - gels and
2. All is well, all is well. Let there be

men re - joice! _____ For to - night dark - ness
peace on earth. _____ Christ is come, go and

fell in - to the dawn of love's light. Sing al -
tell that He is in the man - ger. Sing al -

le, sing al - le - lu - ia! _____
le, sing al - le - lu - ia! _____

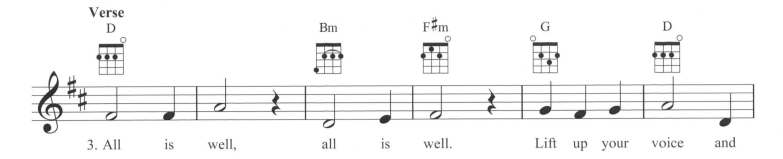

3. All is well, all is well. Lift up your voice and

sing. _____ Born is now Em - man - u - el.

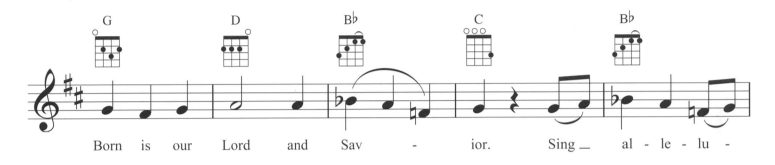

Born is our Lord and Sav - ior. Sing _ al - le - lu -

To Coda **Interlude**

ia! Sing _ al - le - lu - ia! All is well. _____

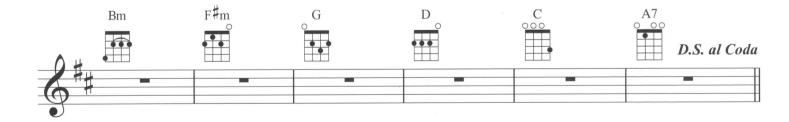

D.S. al Coda

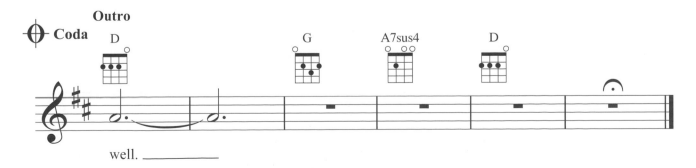

Outro

Coda

well. _____

Almost There

Words and Music by Michael W. Smith, Wes King and Amy Grant

First note

Verse
Freely

| Am | D | Am |

1. Mar - y, full of in - no - cence, car - ry - ing the Ho - ly Prince, you're
(2.) lone - ly road, a will - ing heart, prayer for strength to do your part; you're

| Dsus4 | D | | Am | | D | Am |

al - most there, you're al - most there. Moth - er of the Liv - ing Word,
al - most there, you're al - most there. Trust the Fa - ther to pro - vide

| Dsus4 | D |

trust - ing in the voice you heard, you're al - most there, you're
Bread of Heav - en proph - e - sied; you're al - most there, you're

Chorus

| Am | F | Csus4 | C |

al - most there. You're al - most where ___ the an - gels see re -
al - most there. You're al - most where ___ the wait - ing ends, de -

demp-tion's plan ___ un - fold - ing. All hope is in the
liv - er - ing ___ the life with - in, the an - swered prayer, Em -

Son you'll bear; you're al - most there. 2. A
man - u - el; you're al - most

there. You're al - most where ___ the jour - ney ends, where

death will die and life be - gins, the

an - swered prayer, Em - man - u - el; you're al - most,

al - most there. You're

Chorus

al - most where the wait - ing ends, de -
al - most where your jour - ney ends, where

liv - er - ing the life with - in, } the an - swered prayer, Em -
death will die and life be - gins, }

1.

man - u - el; you're al - most there. You're

2.

man - u - el; you're al - most there.

Angels from the Realms of Glory

Words by James Montgomery
Music by Henry T. Smart

1. An - gels from the realms of glo - ry, wing your flight o'er
2. Shep - herds in the fields a - bid - ing, watch - ing o'er your
3. Sag - es, leave your con - tem - pla - tions; bright - er vi - sions
4. Saints be - fore the al - tar bend - ing, watch - ing long in

all the earth. Ye who sang cre - a - tion's sto - ry
flocks by night, God with man is now re - sid - ing;
beam a - far. Seek the great de - sire of na - tions;
hope and fear, sud - den - ly the Lord, de - scend - ing,

now pro - claim Mes - si - ah's birth.
yon - der shines the ___ in - fant Light.
ye have seen His ___ na - tal star.
in His tem - ple ___ shall ap - pear.

Come and wor - ship!

Come and wor - ship! Wor - ship Christ, the new - born King!

Angels We Have Heard on High

Traditional French Carol
Translated by James Chadwick

First note

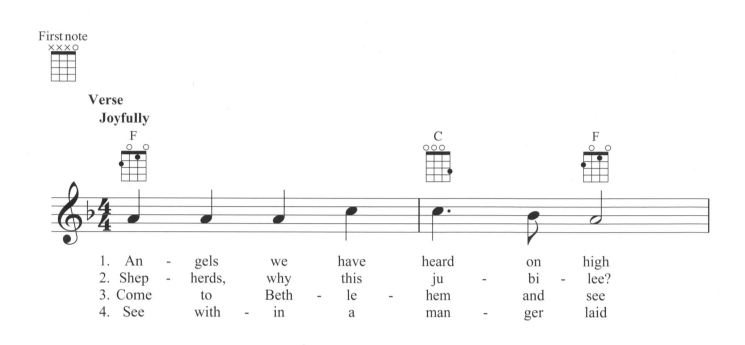

Verse
Joyfully

1. An	-	gels	we	have	heard	on	high
2. Shep	-	herds,	why	this	ju	-	bi	-	lee?
3. Come	to	Beth	-	le	-	hem	and	see
4. See	with	-	in	a	man	-	ger	laid

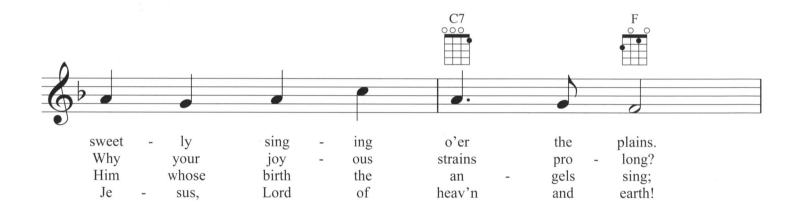

sweet	-	ly	sing	-	ing	o'er	the	plains.
Why	your	joy	-	ous	strains	pro	-	long?
Him	whose	birth	the	an	-	gels	sing;
Je	-	sus,	Lord	of	heav'n	and	earth!

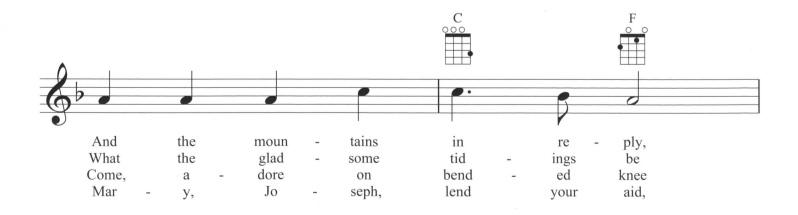

And	the	moun	-	tains	in	re	-	ply,
What	the	glad	-	some	tid	-	ings	be
Come,	a	-	dore	on	bend	-	ed	knee
Mar	-	y,	Jo	-	seph,	lend	your	aid,

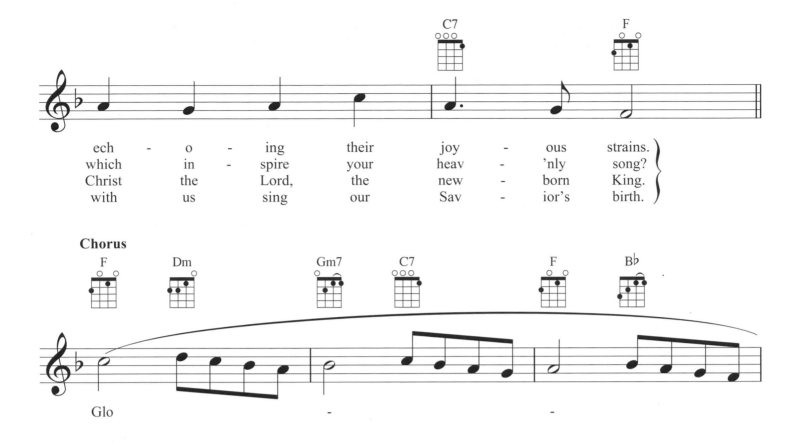

ech - o - ing their joy - ous strains.
which in - spire your heav - 'nly song?
Christ the Lord, the new - born King.
with us sing our Sav - ior's birth.

Chorus

Glo - - -

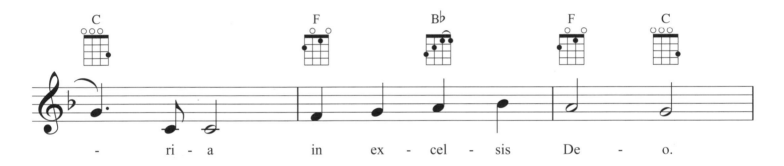

- ri - a in ex - cel - sis De - o.

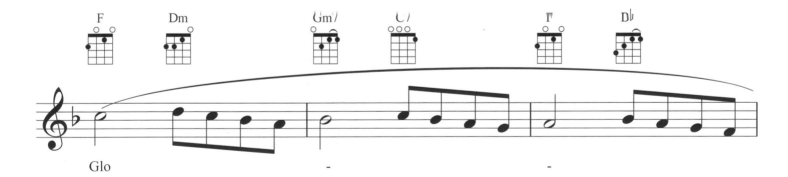

Glo - - -

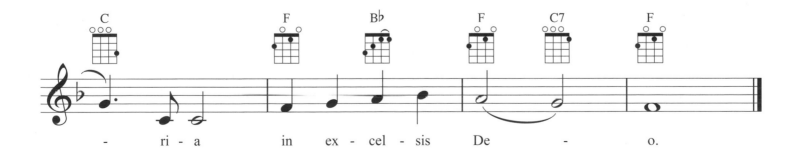

- ri - a in ex - cel - sis De - o.

As Long As There's Christmas

from BEAUTY AND THE BEAST - THE ENCHANTED CHRISTMAS
Music by Rachel Portman
Lyrics by Don Black

look-ing for is some-thing we can't see. _____ Far more pre-cious _____ than

sil-ver and more splen-did _____ than gold, _____ this is some-thing to

treas-ure, _____ but it's some-thing we can't hold. As

𝄋 Chorus

long as there's Christ-mas, I tru-ly be-lieve that

hope is the great-est _____ of the gifts we'll re-ceive, we'll re-

To Coda 1
To Coda 2

ceive. ___ 2. As we all pray to - geth - er, it's a

time ___ to re - joice. ___ And though we ___ may look dif - f'rent, we'll

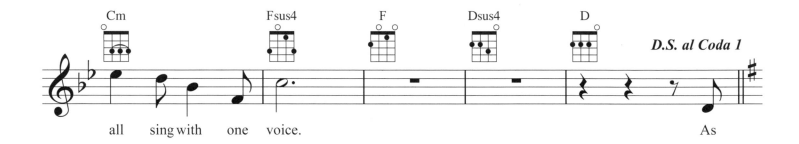

all sing with one voice.   As

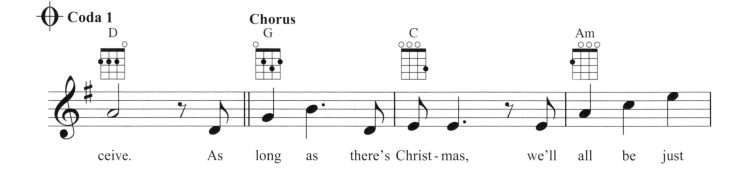

ceive.   As long as there's Christ - mas, we'll all be just

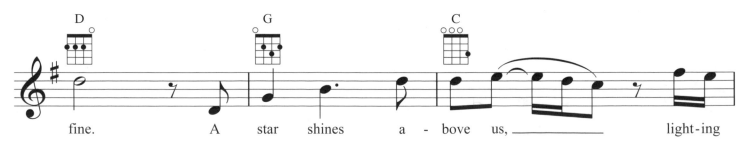

fine.   A star shines a - bove us, _____ light - ing

Away in a Manger

Words by John T. McFarland (v. 3)
Music by James R. Murray

1. A - way in a man - ger, no crib for a bed, the
2. The cat - tle are low - ing, the Ba - by a - wakes, but
3. Be near me, Lord Je - sus, I ask Thee to stay close

lit - tle Lord Je - sus laid down His sweet head. The
lit - tle Lord Je - sus no cry - ing He makes. I
by me for - ev - er and love me, I pray. Bless

stars in the sky ____ looked down where He lay. The
love Thee, Lord Je - sus, look down where from the sky and
all the dear chil - dren in Thy ten - der care and

lit - tle Lord Je - sus, a - sleep on the hay.
stay by my cra - dle 'til morn - ing is nigh.
fit us for heav - en to live with Thee there.

Believe

from Warner Bros. Pictures' THE POLAR EXPRESS
Words and Music by Glen Ballard and Alan Silvestri

There's no time to waste, __ there's so much to cel - e - brate. __ Be -

lieve in what you feel __ in - side __ and give your dreams the wings __ to

fly. You have ev - 'ry - thing you __ need __ if you just __

__ be - lieve. __ be - lieve.

Just __ be - lieve.

Baby, It's Cold Outside

from the Motion Picture NEPTUNE'S DAUGHTER
By Frank Loesser

1. I real - ly can't stay. _____ I've
(2.) sim - ply must go. _____ The

got to go 'way. _____ This eve - ning has been _____
an - swer is "No." _____ The wel - come has been _____

_____ so ver - y nice. _____ My
_____ so nice and warm. _____ My

moth - er will start to wor - ry, and Fa - ther will be pac - ing the
sis - ter will be sus - pi - cious, my broth - er will be there at the

floor. So, real - ly, I'd bet - ter scur - ry. Well,
door. My maid - en aunt's mind is vi - cious. Well,

Because It's Christmas
(For All the Children)

Music by Barry Manilow
Lyric by Bruce Sussman and Jack Feldman

And from a dark __ and frost - ed win - dow, a child __ ap -
to see the smiles __ and hear the laugh - ter; a time __ to

pears to search __ the sky be - cause __ it's
give, a time __ to share be - cause __ it's

1.
Christ - mas, be - cause it's Christ - mas.

2.
Christ - mas for now __ and for - ev - er, for all __ of the

chil - dren and for the chil - dren in us all. _____

The Birthday of a King

Words and Music by William H. Neidlinger

Breath of Heaven
(Mary's Song)

Words and Music by Amy Grant and Chris Eaton

come   and cho - sen me   now _____   to car - ry Your
lone?   Be _____ with me   now, _____   be _____ with me

1.

Bm   Em   Bm   Em

Son.   2. I am now.

𝄋𝄋 **Chorus**

D   Em7   D   Em7   F♯

Breath of heav - en, hold me to - geth - er.   Be for - ev - er

Bm   G   D   Em7

near me, breath of ___ heav - en.   Breath of heav - en, light - en my

D   Em7   F♯   Bm   G

dark - ness.   Pour o - ver me Your   ho - li - ness,   for You are

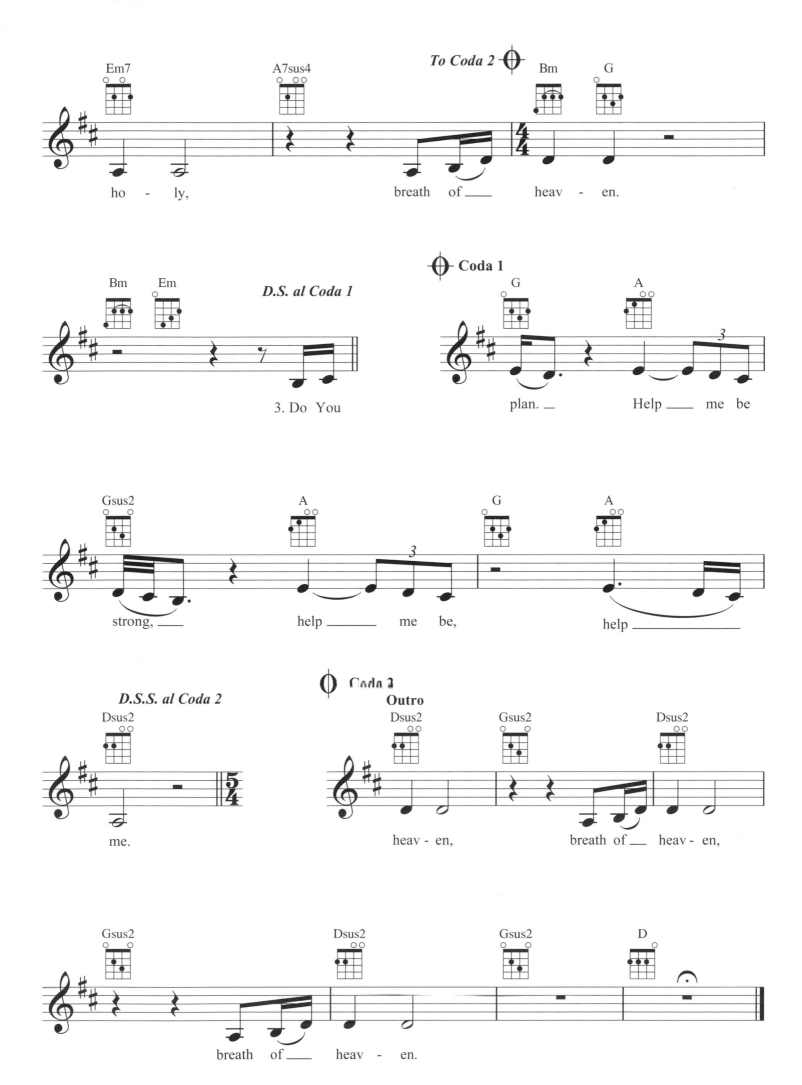

Blue Christmas

Words and Music by Billy Hayes and Jay Johnson

Bring a Torch, Jeannette, Isabella

17th Century French Provençal Carol

First note

Verse
Brightly

1. Bring a torch, ___ Jean - nette, Is - a -
2. *See additional lyrics*

bel - la; bring a torch, ___ come swift - ly and

run. Christ is born, tell the folk of the

vil - lage, Je - sus is sleep - ing in His

cra - dle. Ah, ah, beau - ti - ful

is the Moth - er. Ah, ah,

beau - ti - ful is her Son. _____

Additional Lyrics

2. Hasten now, good folk of the village,
   Hasten now, the Christ Child to see.
   You will find Him asleep in a manger,
   Quietly come and whisper softly.
   Hush, hush, peacefully now He slumbers,
   Hush, hush, peacefully now He sleeps.

A Child Is Born

Music by Thad Jones
Lyrics by Alex Wilder

fawn,   this child is born. _____ One small

Outro-Verse

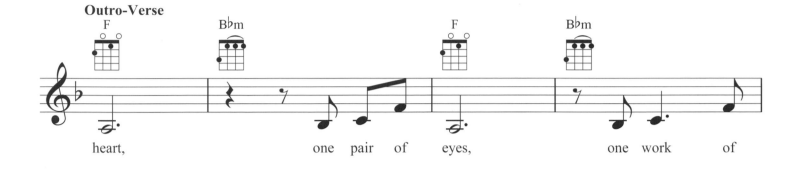

heart,   one pair of eyes,   one work of

art   here in my arms. _____ Here he

lies,   trust - ing ____ and warm,   blessed in ____ this

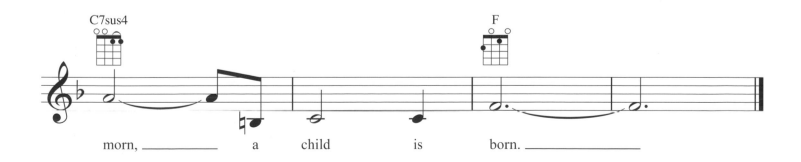

morn, _____ a child is born. _____

Child of God

Words and Music by Grant Cunningham and Matt Huesmann

Christ Is Born

Words and Music by Ray Charles and Domenico Bartolucci

Christmas Auld Lang Syne

Words and Music by Mann Curtis and Frank Military

Christmas Is All in the Heart

Words and Music by Steven Curtis Chapman

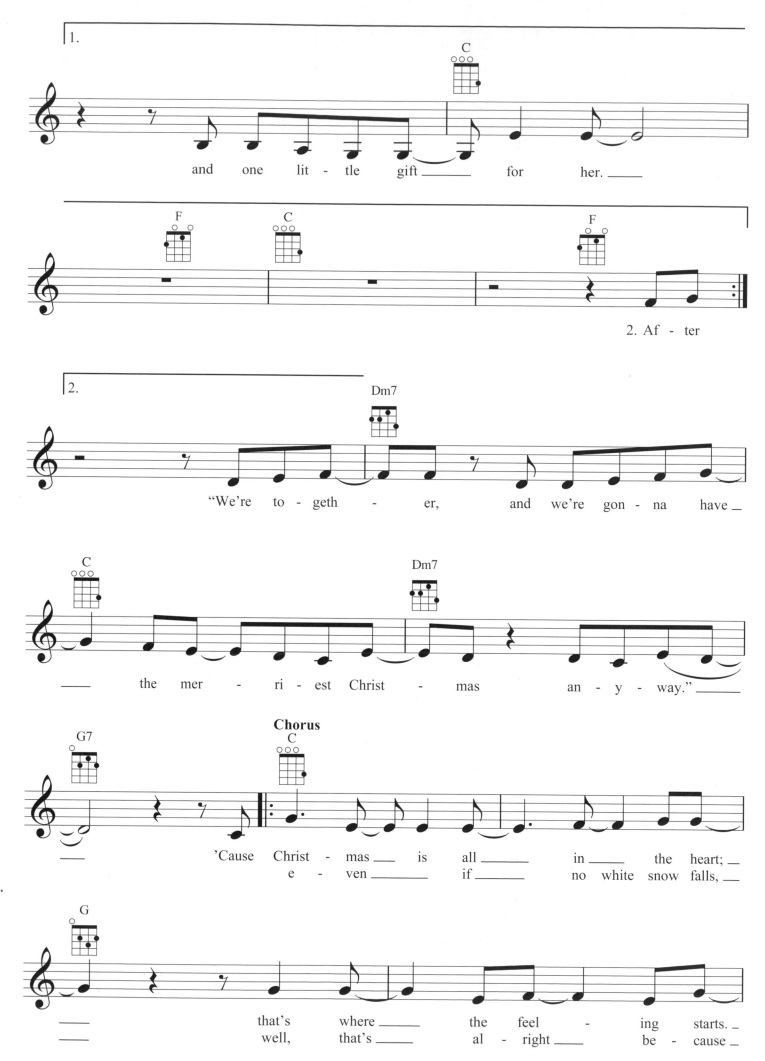

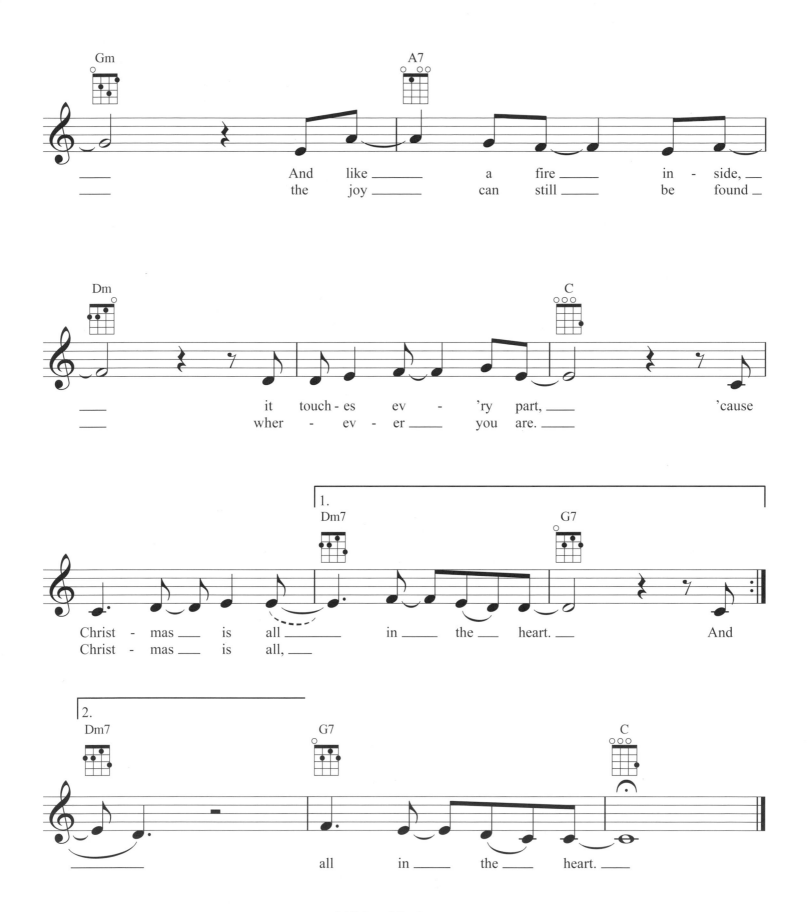

And like _____ a fire _____ in - side, _____
the joy _____ can still _____ be found _____

it touch - es ev - 'ry part, _____ 'cause
wher - ev - er _____ you are. _____

1.
Christ - mas _____ is all _____ in _____ the _____ heart. _____ And
Christ - mas _____ is all, _____

2.
_____ all in _____ the _____ heart. _____

Additional Lyrics

2. After six months on the new job, they're still barely getting by.
   So, in the way of decorations, there's nothing there to catch your eye.
   And both of them would be the first to say,
   "We're together, and we're gonna have the merriest Christmas anyway."

Christmas Is

Lyrics by Spence Maxwell
Music by Percy Faith

First note

Intro
Moderately slow

Christ-mas is sleigh bells,   Christ-mas is shar - ing,

Christ-mas is hol - ly,   Christ-mas is car - ing.

Verse

1. Christ-mas is chil - dren who just can't ___ go to sleep.
2. Christ-mas is car - ols to warm you ___ in the snow.

Christ-mas is mem - 'ries, the kind you ___ al - ways keep.
Christ-mas is bed - time, where no one ___ wants to go.

Deck the halls and ____ give a cheer for all the
All the world is ____ tin - sel bright, so glad to

things that Christ - mas is each year.
know that Christ - mas is to - night.
Christ - mas, ____ mer - ry

Christ - mas, ____ when all your wish - es come true.

1.

2.
true.
Outro
Christ - mas, ____ mer - ry

Christ - mas. ____ May all your wish - es come true.

Christmas Offering

Words and Music by Paul Baloche

Chorus

I bring an of - fer-ing __ of wor - ship to __ my King. __

__ No one on earth __ de - serves __ the prais - es that __ I sing. __

__ Je - sus, may You __ re - ceive __ the hon - or that __ You're due. __

__ Oh, Lord, __ I bring __ an of - fer - ing __ to You. __

I bring an of - fer - ing __ to You. __

Verse

2. The sun __ can - not __ com - pare __ to the glo - ry of __ Your love. __

There is __ no shad - ow in __ Your pres - ence. __

No mor - tal man __ would dare __ to stand __ be - fore __ Your throne, __

be - fore __ the Ho - ly One __ of heav - en. ____ It's

on - ly by __ Your blood, _ and it's on - ly through _ Your mer - cy,

Chorus

Lord, I come. _____ I bring an of -

- fer - ing __ of wor - ship to __ my King. __ No one on earth __

de - serves ___ the prais - es that ___ I sing. ___ Je - sus, may You ___

___ re - ceive ___ the hon - or that ___ You're due. ___ Oh, Lord, ___

1.
___ I bring ___ an of - fer-ing ___ to You. ___

2.
___ I bring ___ an of - fer-ing ___ to You. ___

Outro

_____ Oh, Lord, ___ I bring ___ an of - fer - ing ___ to You. ___

___ Oh, Lord, ___ I bring ___ an of - fer - ing ___ to You. ___

___ I bring an of - fer - ing ___ to You. ___

The Christmas Shoes

Words and Music by Leonard Ahlstrom and Eddie Carswell

1. It was al-most Christ-mas time; there I stood in an-oth-er line, tryin' to buy that last gift or two, not real-ly in the Christ-mas mood. Stand-in' right in front of me was a lit-tle boy wait-ing anx-ious-ly, pac-in' 'round like lit-tle boys do, and in his hands he held a pair of shoes.

(2.) *See additional lyrics*

Pre-Chorus

And his clothes were worn and old, ___ he was dirt - y from head to toe. ___

___ But when it came ___ his time ___ to pay, ___ I

could -n't be - lieve ___ what I heard him say. "Sir, I wan - na

Chorus

buy these shoes ___ for my ma - ma, please. ___ It's

Christ - mas Eve ___ and these shoes are just her ___ size. Could you

hur - ry, sir? ___ Dad - dy says there's not much time. ___ You see,

she's been sick for quite __ a while, __ and I know these shoes will make __

__ her smile, __ and I want her to look beau - ti - ful __ if

To Coda

1.

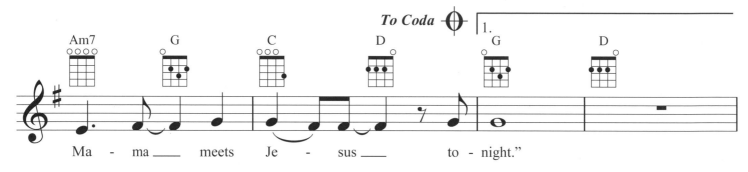

Ma - ma __ meets Je - sus __ to - night."

2.

2. They count - ed night." _____ I knew I

Bridge

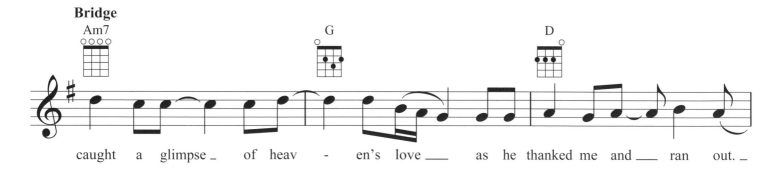

caught a glimpse _ of heav - en's love __ as he thanked me and __ ran out. _

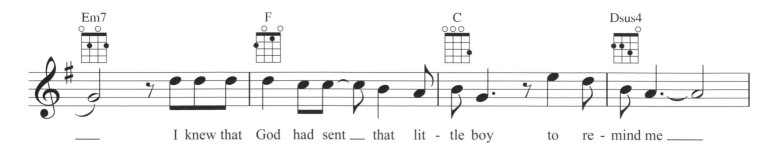

__ I knew that God had sent __ that lit - tle boy to re - mind me __

50

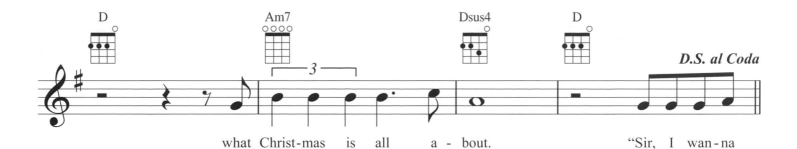

what Christ-mas is all a-bout.   "Sir, I wan-na

Coda

Outro

night.   I want her to ____ look beau-

-ti-ful   if Ma - ma ___ meets Je - sus _____ to-

night." _____

Additional Lyrics

2. They counted pennies for what seemed like years,
   Then the cashier said, "Son, there's not enough here."
   He searched his pockets frantically,
   Then he turned and he looked at me.
   He said, "Mama made Christmas good at our house,
   Though most years she just did without.
   Tell me, sir, what am I gonna do?
   Somehow I've gotta buy her these Christmas shoes.

Pre-Chorus: So, I laid the money down. I just had to help him out.
   And I'll never forget the look on his face when he said,
   "Mama's gonna look so great."

The Christmas Song
(Chestnuts Roasting on an Open Fire)

Music and Lyric by Mel Tormé and Robert Wells

Chest-nuts roast-ing on an o-pen fire, Jack Frost nip-ping at your nose. Yule-tide car-ols be-ing sung by a choir and folks dressed up like Es-ki-mos. Ev-'ry-bod-y knows a tur-key and some mis-tle-toe help to make the sea-son bright. Ti-ny tots with their eyes all a-glow will find it hard to sleep to-night. They know that

Bridge

Gm7   C7   Gm7   C7   Gm7   C7

San - ta's on his way.   He's load - ed   lots of toys and good - ies on his

Fmaj7   Fm7   Bb7

sleigh.   And ev - 'ry moth - er's child _____ is gon - na

Eb   Am   D7   Dm7   G7

spy _____ to see if rein - deer real - ly know how to fly.   And

Outro-Verse

C   Dm7   Cmaj7   G7

so, I'm of - fer - ing this sim - ple phrase to

C   C7   F   E7   Am   Fm6

kids from one to nine - ty - two.   Al - though it's been said man - y

C   B7   C   Am   Dm7   G7   C

times, man - y ways, "Mer - ry Christ - mas to you."

The Christmas Waltz

Words by Sammy Cahn
Music by Jule Styne

Verse

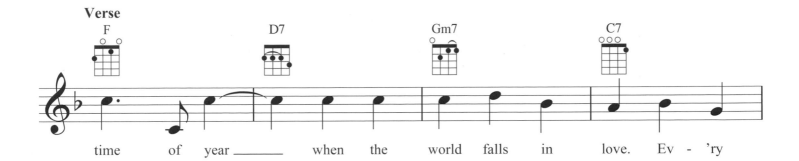

time   of   year _____   when   the   world   falls   in   love.   Ev - 'ry

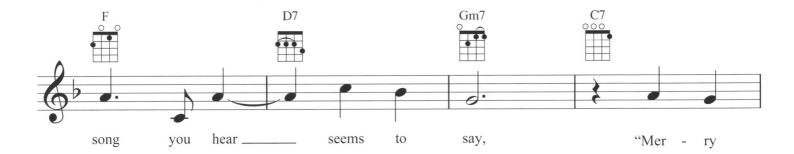

song   you   hear _____   seems   to   say,   "Mer - ry

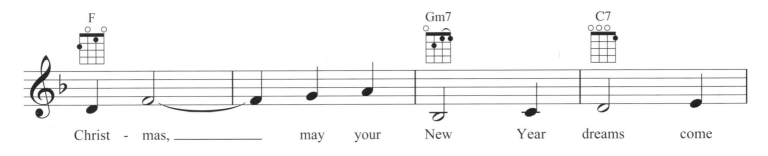

Christ - mas, _____   may   your   New   Year   dreams   come

Outro

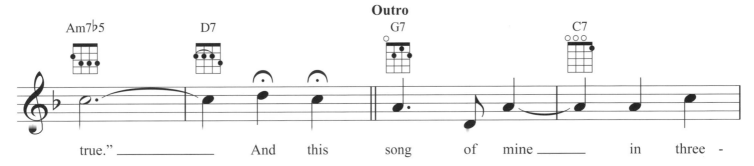

true." _____   And   this   song   of   mine _____   in   three -

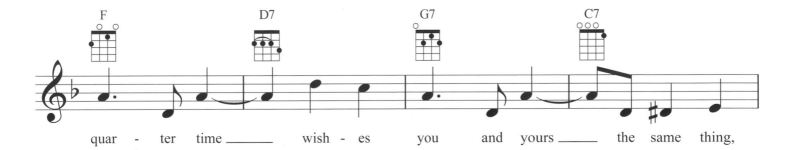

quar - ter   time _____   wish - es   you   and   yours _____   the   same   thing,

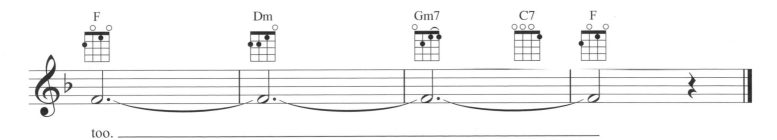

too. _____

Christmastime

Words and Music by Michael W. Smith and Joanna Carlson

Christmas Time Is Here

from A CHARLIE BROWN CHRISTMAS
Words by Lee Mendelson
Music by Vince Guaraldi

Cold December Nights

Words and Music by Shawn Stockman and Michael McCary

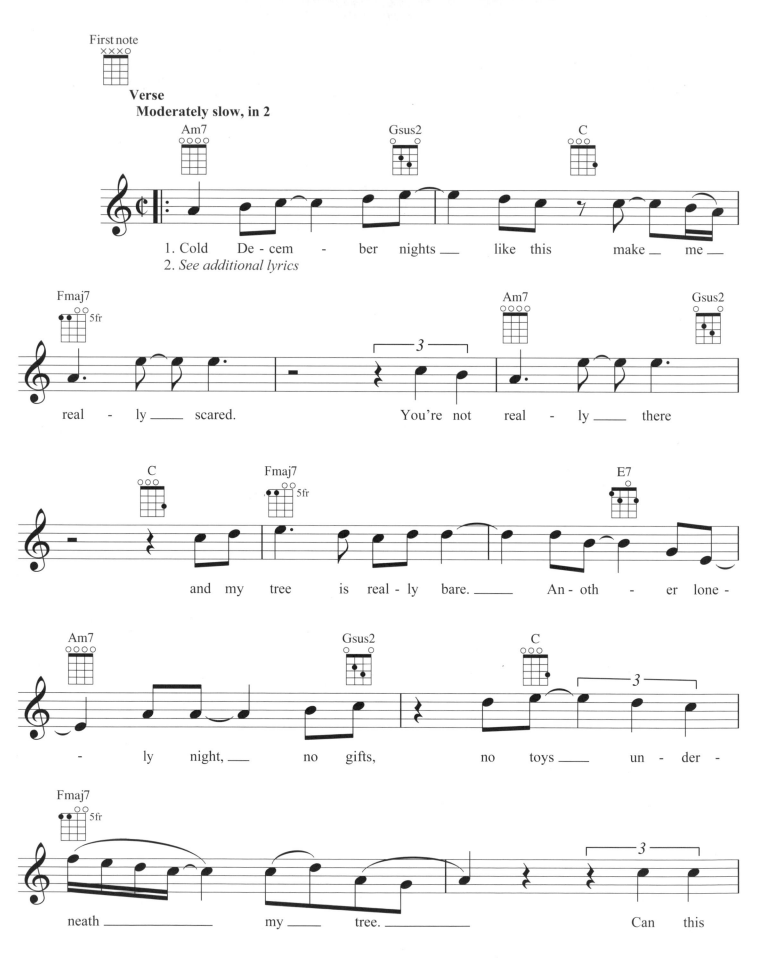

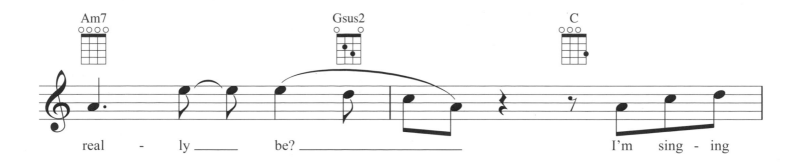

real - ly _____ be? _____ I'm sing - ing

Christ - mas car - ols and there's no Christ - mas for

Chorus

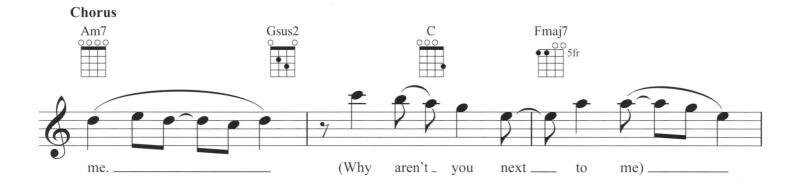

me. _____ (Why aren't _ you next _____ to me) _____

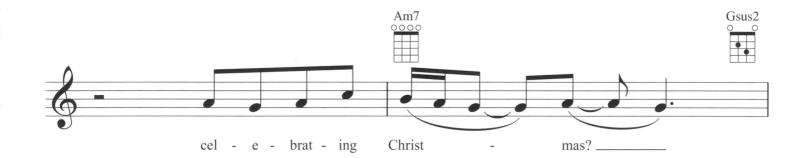

cel - e - brat - ing Christ - mas? _____

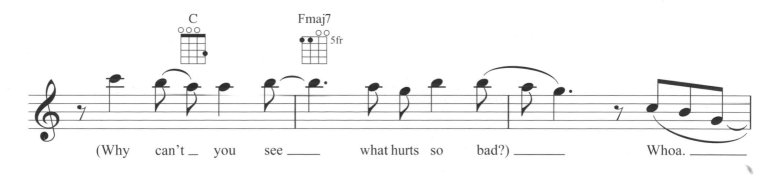

(Why can't _ you see _____ what hurts so bad?) _____ Whoa. _____

How ___ can you go _____ with - out ___ pay- ing mind ___

___ to my sor - row _____ (You can't i - mag -

- ine how, how I feel.) _____ on this cold ___ De - cem - ber night? ___

Additional Lyrics

2. The stars shine bright as the night air,
   And the thought of you not being here makes me shed a tear.
   And yet, matters remain unclear 'bout why you're gone,
   Or if you'll ever return to this broken heart.
   Life is so torn apart, and God knows,
   God knows where I need to start rebuilding.

Coventry Carol

Words by Robert Croo
Traditional English Melody

Additional Lyrics

3. Herod the king, in his raging,
   Charged he hath this day
   His men of might, in his own sight,
   All young children to slay.

4. That woe is me, poor Child, for Thee!
   And ever morn and day,
   For Thy parting neither say nor sing,
   By, by, lully, lullay.

Do You Hear What I Hear

Words and Music by Noel Regney and Gloria Shayne

D.S. al Coda

kite.   2., 3. Said the   4. Said the

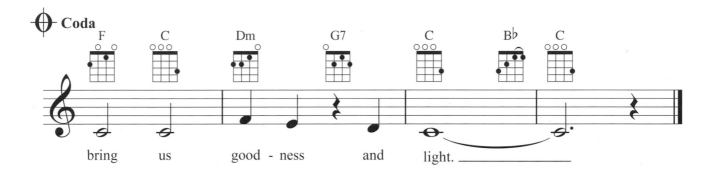

bring us good - ness and light. _____

Additional Lyrics

2. Said the little lamb to the shepherd boy:
   Do you hear what I hear?
   Ringing through the sky, shepherd boy,
   Do you hear what I hear?
   A song, a song, high above the tree,
   With a voice as big as the sea,
   With a voice as big as the sea.

3. Said the shepherd boy to the mighty king:
   Do you know what I know?
   In your palace warm, mighty king,
   Do you know what I know?
   A Child, a Child shivers in the cold;
   Let us bring Him silver and gold,
   Let us bring Him silver and gold.

4. Said the king to the people ev'rywhere:
   Listen to what I say!
   Pray for peace, people ev'rywhere.
   Listen to what I say!
   The Child, the Child, sleeping in the night,
   He will bring us goodness and light,
   He will bring us goodness and light.

Emmanuel
(Hallowed Manger Ground)
Words and Music by Chris Tomlin and Ed Cash

1. What hope we hold ___ this star - lit night: ___ a King is born ___ in Beth - le - hem. ___ Our jour - ney long, ___ we seek the light ___ that leads to the hal - low - ed man - ger ground.

2. What fear we felt ___ in the si - lent age. ___ Four
(3.) Son of God ___ here born to bleed; ___ a

hun - dred years; ____ can He be found? ____ But
crown of thorns ____ would He pierce His brow. ____ And

To Coda 1

bro - ken by _____ a ba - by's cry, _____ re -
we be - held _____ this of - fer - ing, _____ ex -

joice in the hal - low - ed man - ger ground. Em -

%. %. Chorus

man - u - el, Em - man - u - el,

God in - car - nate, here to dwell. Em -

man - u - el, Em - man - u - el,

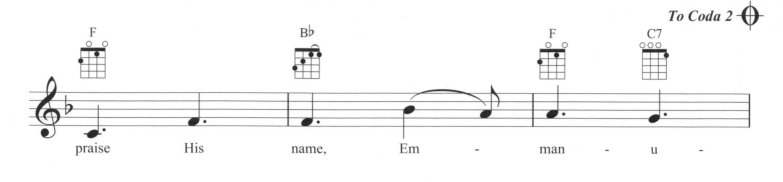

praise   His   name,   Em - man - u -

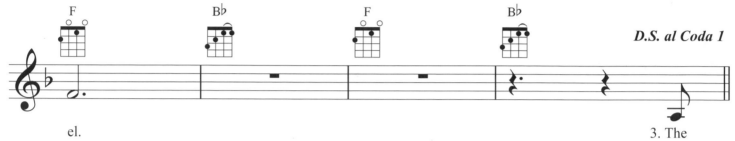

D.S. al Coda 1

el.   3. The

⊕ **Coda 1**

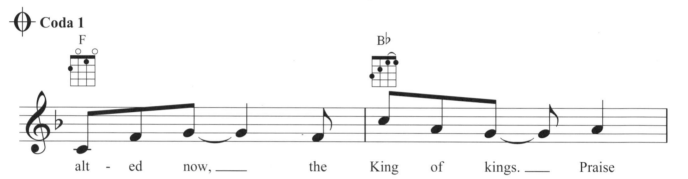

alt - ed   now, _____ the   King   of   kings. _____ Praise

D.S.S. al Coda 2

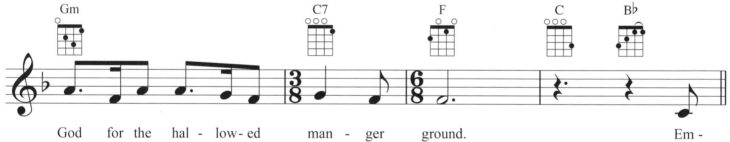

God   for the   hal - low- ed   man - ger   ground.   Em -

⊕ **Coda 2**   **Outro**

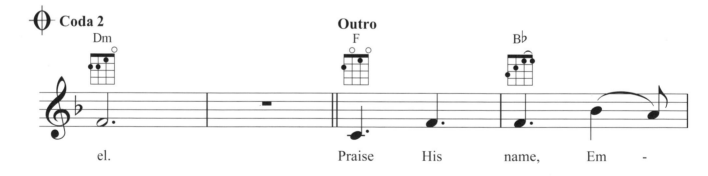

el.   Praise   His   name,   Em -

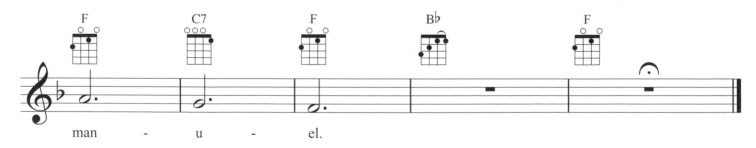

man - u -   el.

Dance of the Sugar Plum Fairy

from THE NUTCRACKER SUITE, OP. 71A
By Pyotr Il'yich Tchaikovsky

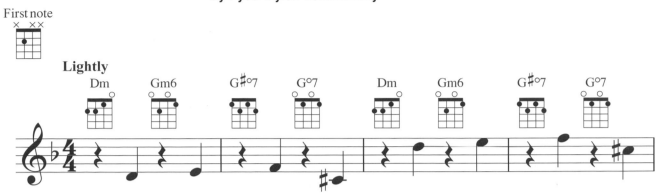

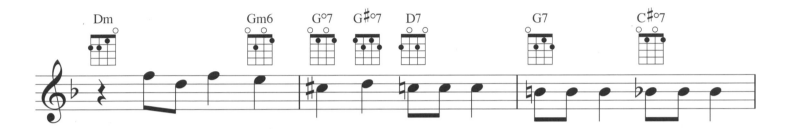

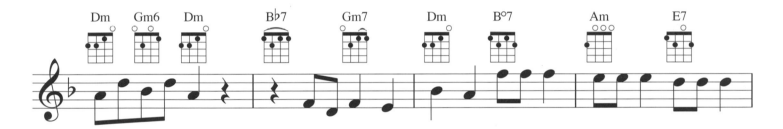

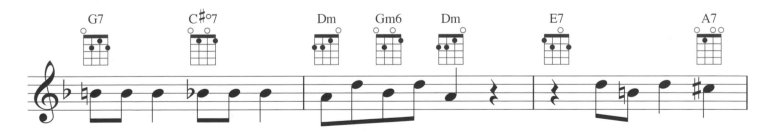

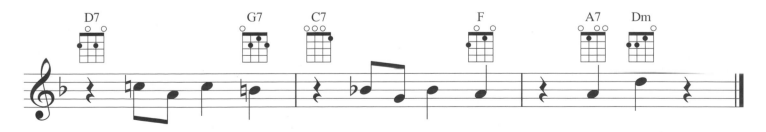

Fairytale of New York

Words and Music by Jeremy Finer and Shane MacGowan

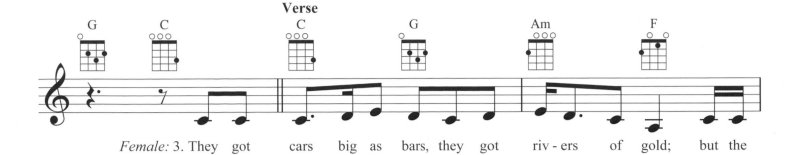

Verse

Female: 3. They got cars big as bars, they got riv - ers of gold; but the

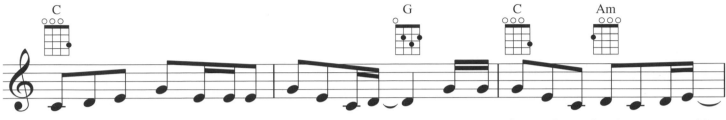

wind goes right through you, it's no place for the old. __ When you first took my hand on a cold __

__ Christ - mas Eve, you prom - ised me Broad - way was wait - ing for me. __ 4. You were

Verse

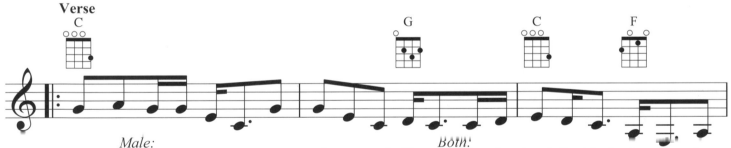

Male: hand - some. You were pret - ty, Queen of New York Cit - y. *Both:* When the band fin - ished play - ing, they

(5.) *See additional lyrics*

howled out for more. _ Si - na - tra was swing - ing; all the drunks, they were sing - ing. We

Chorus

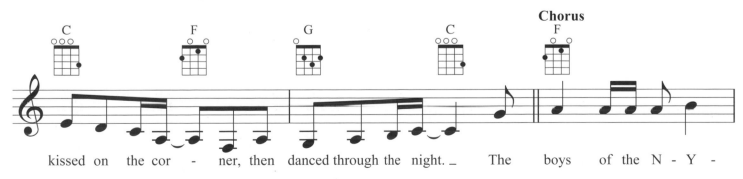

kissed on the cor - ner, then danced through the night. _ The boys of the N - Y -

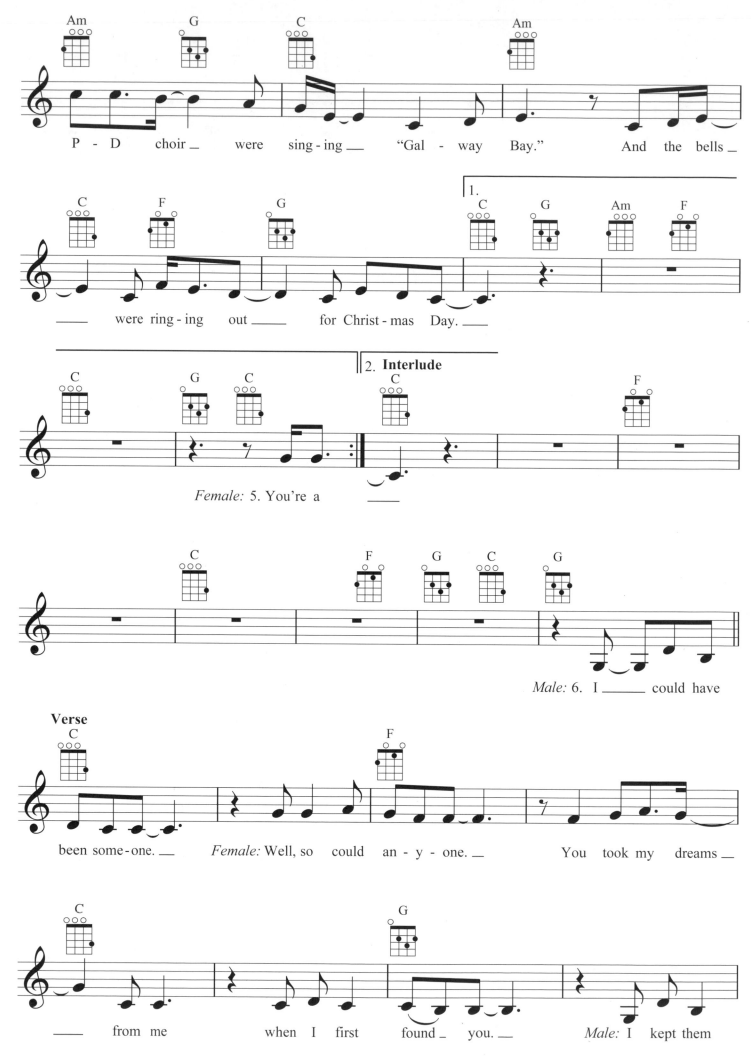

P - D choir ___ were sing - ing ___ "Gal - way Bay." And the bells _

___ were ring - ing out ___ for Christ - mas Day. ___

2. Interlude

Female: 5. You're a ___

Male: 6. I ___ could have

Verse

been some - one. ___ *Female:* Well, so could an - y - one. ___ You took my dreams _

___ from me when I first found _ you. ___ *Male:* I kept them

with me, babe; ___ I put them with my own. ___ Can't ___ make it

all a - lone; ___ I've built ___ my dreams a - round you.

Outro-Chorus

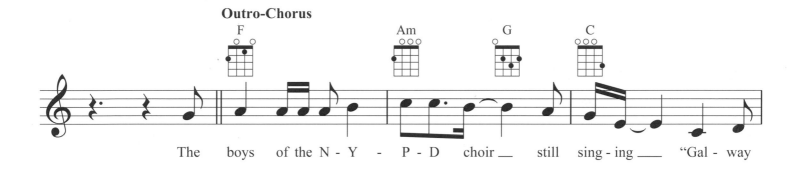

The boys of the N - Y - P - D choir ___ still sing - ing ___ "Gal - way

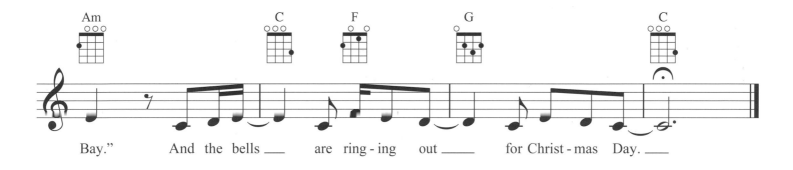

Bay." And the bells ___ are ring - ing out ____ for Christ - mas Day. ___

Additional Lyrics

2. Got on a lucky one, came in eighteen to one;
   I've got a feeling this year's for me and you.
   So happy Christmas; I love you, baby.
   I can see a better time when all our dreams come true.

5. *(Female)* You're a bum, you're a punk!
   (Male) You're an old slut on junk,
   Lying there almost dead on a drip in that bed!
   (Female) You scumbag! You maggot!
   You cheap, lousy faggot!
   Happy Christmas, your arse!
   I pray God it's our last.

The First Noel

17th Century English Carol
Music from W. Sandys' *Christmas Carols*

1. The __ first _____ No - el the __ an - gel did

(2.–5.) See additional lyrics

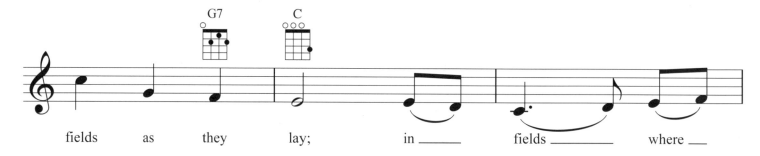

say, was to cer - tain poor shep - herds in

fields as they lay; in ___ fields _____ where __

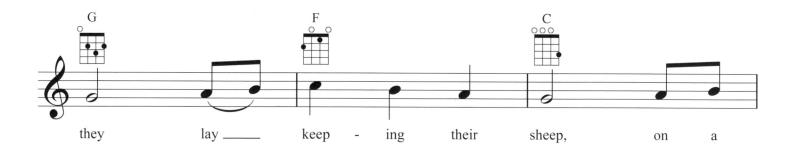

they lay ____ keep - ing their sheep, on a

cold win - ter's night ____ that was ___ so deep. No -

Chorus

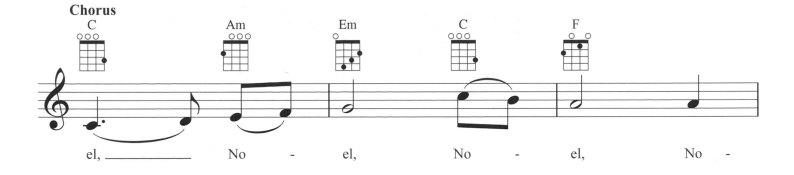

el, _____ No - el, No - el, No -

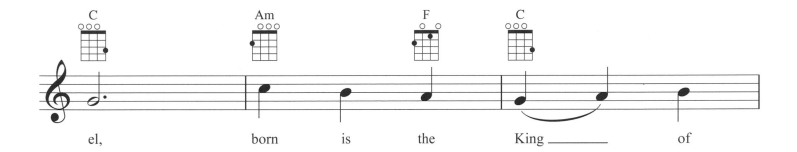

el, born is the King _____ of

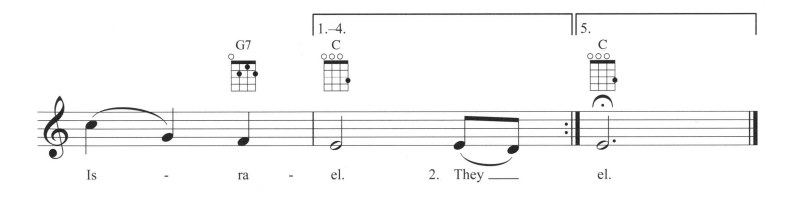

Is - ra - el. 2. They _____ el.

Additional Lyrics

2. They looked up and saw a star
   Shining in the east, beyond them far;
   And to the earth it gave great light
   And so it continued both day and night.

3. And by the light of that same star,
   Three wise men came from country far;
   To seek for a King was their intent,
   And to follow the star wherever it went.

4. This star drew nigh to the northwest,
   O'er Bethlehem it took its rest;
   And there it did both stop and stay,
   Right over the place where Jesus lay.

5. Then entered in those wise men three,
   Full reverently upon their knee;
   And offered there in His presence,
   Their gold and myrrh and frankincense.

The Friendly Beasts

Traditional English Carol

First note

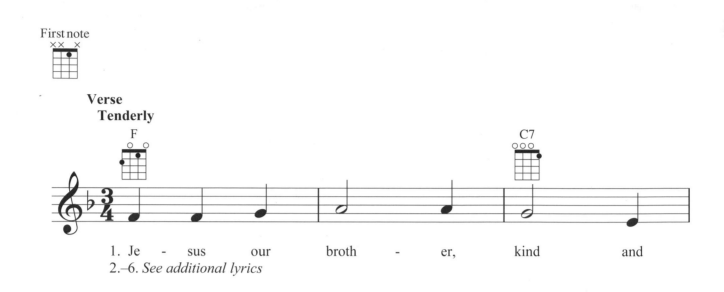

Verse
Tenderly

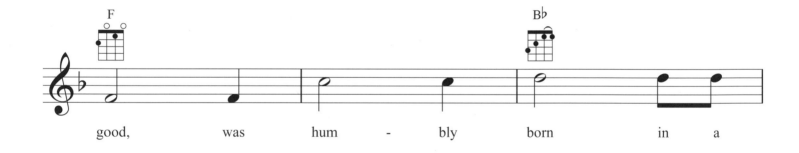

1. Je - sus our broth - er, kind and
2.–6. *See additional lyrics*

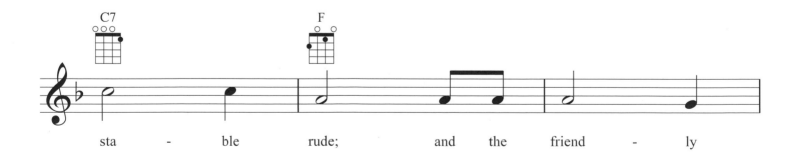

good, was hum - bly born in a

sta - ble rude; and the friend - ly

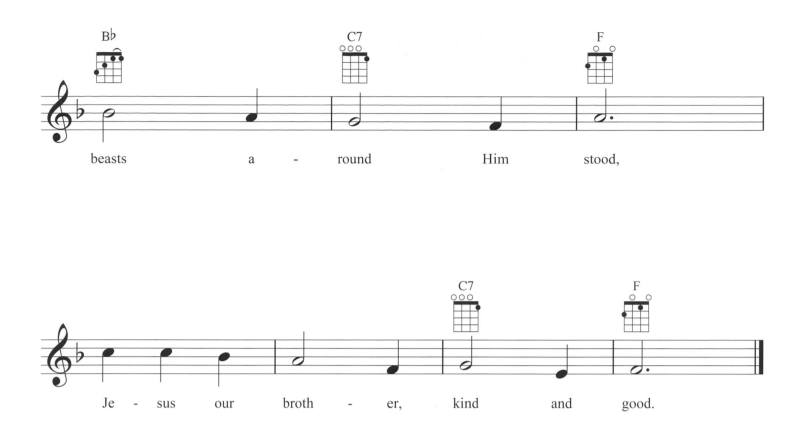

beasts   a - round   Him   stood,

Je - sus   our   broth - er,   kind   and   good.

Additional Lyrics

2. "I," said the donkey, shaggy and brown,
   "I carried His mother up hill and down.
   I carried His mother to Bethlehem town."
   "I," said the donkey, shaggy and brown.

3. "I," said the cow, all white and red,
   "I gave Him my manger for His bed.
   I gave Him my hay to pillow His head."
   "I," said the cow, all white and red.

4. "I," said the sheep with the curly horn,
   "I gave Him my wool for His blanket warm.
   He wore my coat on Christmas morn."
   "I," said the sheep with the curly horn.

5. "I," said the dove from the rafters high,
   "I cooed Him to sleep that He would not cry.
   We cooed Him to sleep, my mate and I."
   "I," said the dove from the rafters high.

6. Thus every beast by some good spell,
   In the stable dark was glad to tell
   Of the gift he gave Emmanuel,
   The gift he gave Emmanuel.

Gesù Bambino
(The Infant Jesus)

Text by Frederick H. Martens
Music by Pietro Yon

The Gift

Words and Music by Tom Douglas and Jim Brickman

Chorus

All I want ___ is to hold ___ you for -
ev - er. ___ All I need ___ is you more ___ ev - 'ry day. ___
You saved my heart ___ from be - ing
bro - ken a - part. You gave your love a - way and I'm thank - ful
ev - 'ry day ___ for the gift.

Additional Lyrics

2. Watching as you softly sleep, what I'd give if I could keep
Just this moment, if only time stood still.
But the colors fade away and the years will make us gray.
But, baby, in my eyes you'll still be beautiful.

Happy Xmas
(War Is Over)

Written by John Lennon and Yoko Ono

1. So, this is X - mas, and what have you
(2., 3.) *See additional lyrics*

done? An - oth - er year o - ver, a new one just be -

gun. And so this is X - mas; I hope you have

fun, the near and the dear ones, the old and the

young. A mer - ry, mer - ry X - mas and a hap - py New

To Coda

Year.   Let's hope it's a   good one _____   with - out   an - y

2nd time, D.S. al Coda

Coda

fear.   2., 3. And so, this is

fear.

Outro

War   is   o - ver   if   you   want   it.

War   is   o - ver   now. _____

Additional Lyrics

2. And so, this is Xmas for weak and for strong,
   The rich and the poor ones; the road is so long.
   And so, happy Xmas for black and for white,
   For the yellow and red ones; let's stop all the fights.

3. And so, this is Xmas, and what have we done?
   Another year over, a new one just begun.
   And so, happy Xmas; we hope you have fun,
   The near and the dear ones, the old and the young.

Hark! The Herald Angels Sing

Words by Charles Wesley
Altered by George Whitefield
Music by Felix Mendelssohn-Bartholdy
Arranged by William H. Cummings

First note

Verse
Moderately

1. Hark! the her - ald an - gels sing, _____
2. Christ, by high - est heav'n a - dored, _____
3. Hail, the heav'n - born Prince of Peace! _____

"Glo - ry to the new - born King!
Christ, the ev - er - last - ing Lord!
Hail, the Son of right - eous - ness!

Peace on earth, and mer - cy mild, _____ God and sin - ners
Late in time be - hold Him come, _____ off - spring of the
Light and life to all He brings, _____ ris'n with heal - ing

rec - on - ciled." Joy - ful, all ye na - tions rise, _____
vir - gin's womb. Veil'd in flesh the God - head see, _____
in His wings. Mild He lays His glo - ry by, _____

F   B♭   C

join   the   tri -   umph   of   the   skies. _____

hail   th'in -   car -   nate   De -   i -   ty. _____

born   that   man   no   more   may   die. _____

B♭   D   Gm

With   th'an -   gel -   ic   hosts   pro -   claim,

Pleased   as   man   with   man   to   dwell,

Born   to   raise   the   sons   of   earth,

C7   F   C7   F

"Christ   is _____ born   in   Beth -   le -   hem." ⎫

Je -   sus, _____ our   Im -   man -   u -   el. ⎬

born   to _____ give   them   sec -   ond   birth. ⎭

Chorus

B♭   D   Gm

Hark!   the   her -   ald   an -   gels   sing,

C7   F   **1., 2.**   C7   F   **3.**   C7   F

"Glo - ry _____ to   the   new - born   King!"   new - born   King!"

Have Yourself a Merry Little Christmas

from MEET ME IN ST. LOUIS
Words and Music by Hugh Martin and Ralph Blane

Outro-Verse

Here with Us

Words and Music by Joy Elizabeth Williams, Ben Glover and Jason D. Ingram

1. It's still a mys-ter-y ___ to me ___ that the hands ___ of God ___ could be so small, ___ how ti-ny fin-gers reach-ing in ___ the night ___ were the ver-y hands ___ that meas-ured ___ the sky. ___

Chorus

___ Hal-le-lu-jah, hal-le-lu-jah! Heav-en's love ___

_____ reach - ing down _ to save the world. Hal - le - lu - jah, hal - le -

lu - jah! Son of God, serv - ant King, _ here with

us, You're here with us. Mmm. _____

Verse

_____ 2. Still a mys - ter - y _____ to me, _____ oh, _____

_____ how His in - fant eyes _ had seen the dawn _ of time, _____

how His ears _ had heard _ an an - gel sym - pho - ny; _

D.S. al Coda

but still, Mar - y had __ to rock __ her Sav - ior __ to sleep. __ Hal - le -

Coda

Interlude

us,   You're   here   with   us.

Mmm _____ la la la la la la la.   Oh. _____

__   You're   here. _____   La la la la

la la la la la la la la la   la   la.

Verse

3. Je - sus   the   Christ, __

born in Beth - le - hem, __ a ba - by born __ to save, __ to

save the souls __ of men. _____ Hal - le -

Chorus

lu - jah, hal - le - lu - jah! Heav - en's love __ reach - ing down __ to save the

world. Hal - le - lu - jah, hal - le - lu - jah! Son of

God, serv - ant King, __ here with us. _____ Oh, hal - le - us, You're here with

Outro

us, You're here with us. _____

The Holly and the Ivy

18th Century English Carol

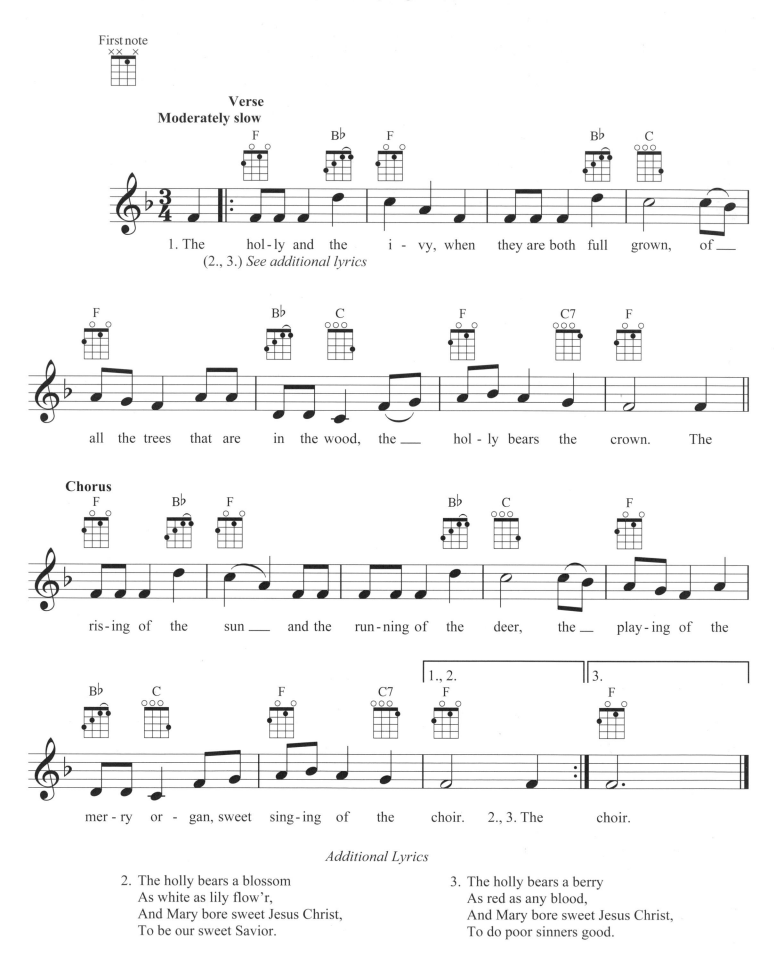

Additional Lyrics

2. The holly bears a blossom
   As white as lily flow'r,
   And Mary bore sweet Jesus Christ,
   To be our sweet Savior.

3. The holly bears a berry
   As red as any blood,
   And Mary bore sweet Jesus Christ,
   To do poor sinners good.

Grown-Up Christmas List

Words and Music by David Foster and Linda Thompson-Jenner

First note

Verse
Moderately slow

C G Am Em7 F

1. Do you re-mem-ber me? I sat up-on _____ your knee. _____ I

C Dm7 G7sus4 G7

wrote to you with child - hood fan - ta - sies. 2. Well,

Verse

C G Am Em7 F

I'm all grown _ up now and still need help some - how. I'm
(3) chil-dren, we be - lieved the grand - est sight to see was

C Dm7 G7sus4 G7

not a child, _ but my heart still can dream. So,
some - thing love - ly wrapped be - neath our tree. Well,

C G Am Em7 F

here's my life - long wish, my grown - up Christ - mas list, not
heav - en sure - ly knows that pack - ag - es and bows can

for my-self, ___ but for a world ___ in need.
nev - er heal ___ a hurt-ing hu - man soul.

𝄋 Chorus

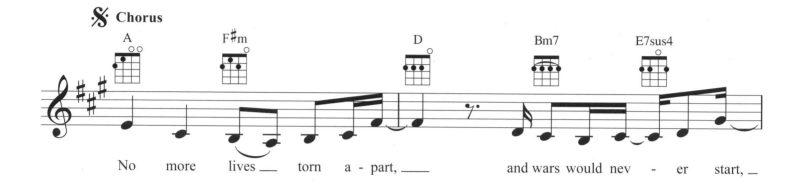

No more lives ___ torn a - part, ___ and wars would nev - er start, ___

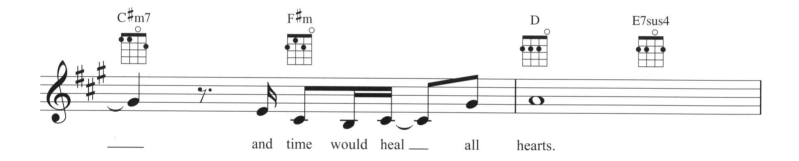

___ and time would heal ___ all hearts.

And ev - 'ry - one would have ___ a friend, ___ and right would al - ways

win, and love would nev - er end. _____

This is my grown - up Christ - mas list.

3. As

list. _____

Bridge

What is ____ this il - lu - sion called? The in - no - cence of youth. __ May - be

on - ly in ____ our blind be - lief ____ can we ev - er find __ the truth.

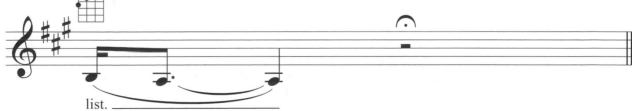

list. _____

Home
(When Shadows Fall)

Words and Music by Geoff Clarkson, Harry Clarkson and Peter Van Steeden

Eve - ning marks the close of day;
Eve - ning ev - er brings to me

skies of blue be - gin to gray, crim - son hues are
dreams of days that used to be, mem - o - ries of

1.
fad - ing in the west.

2.
those I love the best.

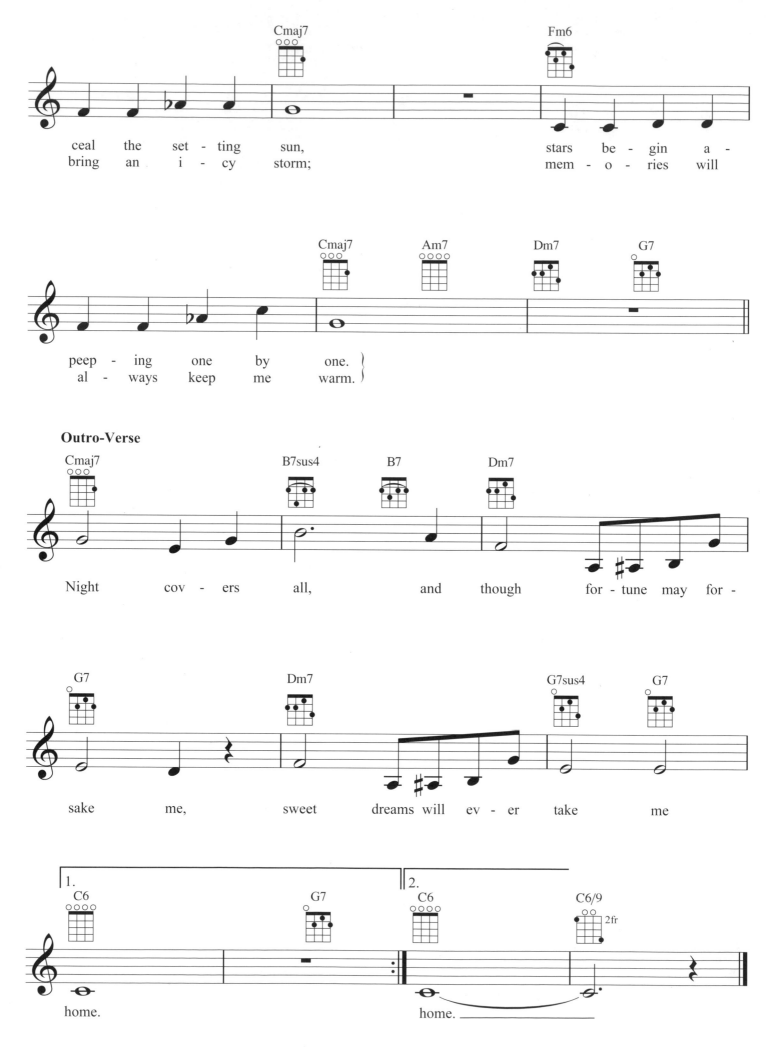

Outro-Verse

I Heard the Bells on Christmas Day

Words by Henry Wadsworth Longfellow
Adapted by Johnny Marks
Music by Johnny Marks

(There's No Place Like)
Home for the Holidays

Words and Music by Al Stillman and Robert Allen

First note

Verse

Moderately, in 2

Oh, there's no place like home for the hol - i - days, ___ ___ 'cause no mat - ter how far a - way you roam, ___ ___ when you pine for the sun - shine of a friend - ly gaze, ___ ___ for the hol - i - days you can't beat home, sweet home.

Bridge

I met a man who lives in Ten - nes - see, and he was head - in' for Penn - syl - va - nia and some home - made pump - kin pie.

From Penn - syl - va - nia folks are trav - 'lin' down to Dix - ie's sun - ny

shores. From At - lan - tic to Pa - cif - ic, gee, the traf - fic is ter -

Outro-Verse

rif - ic. Oh, there's no place like home for the hol - i - days, _____

_____ 'cause no mat - ter how far a - way you roam, _____

_____ if you want to be hap - py in a mil - lion ways, _____

1. _____ for the hol - i - days you can't beat home, sweet home. _____ Oh, there's

2. can't beat home, sweet home. _____

I Wonder as I Wander

By John Jacob Niles

First note

Verse
Expressively

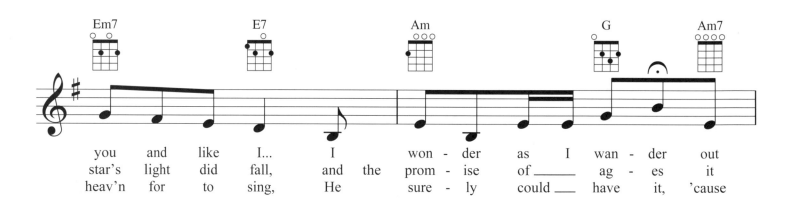

1., 4. I won - der as I wan - der out un - der the sky, how
(2.) Mar - y birthed _ Je - sus, 'twas in a cow's stall, with
(3.) Je - sus had ___ want - ed for an - y wee thing, a

Je - sus the Sav - ior did come for to die for poor on - 'ry peo - ple like
wise men and farm - ers and shep - herds and all. But high from God's heav - en a
star in the sky or a bird on the wing, or all of God's an - gels in

you and like I... I won - der as I wan - der out
star's light did fall, and the prom - ise of ____ ag - es it
heav'n for to sing, He sure - ly could ___ have it, 'cause

1.–3.

un - der the sky. 2. When
then did re - call. 3. If
He was the King. 4. I

4.

un - der the sky.

In the Bleak Midwinter

Poem by Christina Rossetti
Music by Gustav Holst

I'll Be Home for Christmas

Words and Music by Kim Gannon and Walter Kent

First note

Chorus
Slowly, in 2

I'll be home for Christ - mas. ___

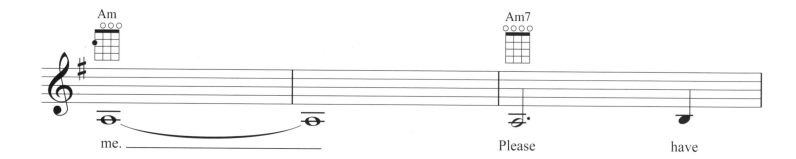

___ You can plan on

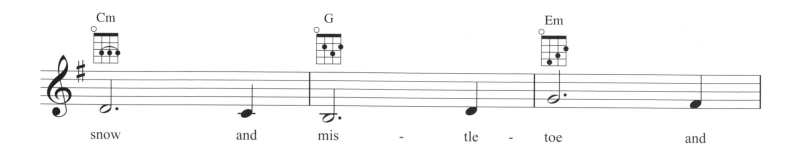

me. ___ Please have

snow and mis - tle - toe and

Infant Holy, Infant Lowly

Traditional Polish Carol
Paraphrased by Edith M.G. Reed

1. In-fant Ho-ly, In-fant low-ly, for His bed a cat-tle
(2.) sleep-ing, shep-herds keep-ing vig-il 'til the morn-ing

stall. Ox-en low-ing, lit-tle know-ing Christ the
new. Saw the glo-ry, heard the sto-ry, tid-ings

Babe is Lord of all. Swift are wing-ing an-gels
of a Gos-pel true. Thus re-joic-ing, free from

sing-ing, no-els ring-ing, tid-ings bring-ing: Christ the
sor-row, prais-es voic-ing, greet the mor-row: Christ the

Babe is Lord of all! 2. Flocks are
Babe was born for you.

It Must Have Been the Mistletoe
(Our First Christmas)

Words and Music by Justin Wilde and Doug Konecky

1. It must have been the mis - tle - toe, the
(2., 3.) *See additional lyrics*

la - zy fire, the fall - ing snow, the mag - ic in the frost - y air, that

feel - ing ev - 'ry - where. It must have been the pret - ty lights that

glis - tened in the si - lent night, or may - be just the stars so bright that

Coda 2

must have been the mis-tle-toe. It

Outro

must have been the mis-tle-toe. It must have been the

mis-tle-toe.

Additional Lyrics

2. It could have been the holiday, the midnight ride upon a sleigh,
   The countryside all dressed in white, that crazy snowball fight.
   It could have been the steeple bell that wrapped us up within its spell.
   It only took one kiss to know; it must have been the mistletoe.

3. It must have been the mistletoe, the lazy fire, the falling snow,
   The magic in the frosty air that made me love you.
   On Christmas Eve a wish came true that night I fell in love with you.
   It only took one kiss to know; it must have been the mistletoe.

It Came Upon the Midnight Clear

Words by Edmund Hamilton Sears
Music by Richard Storrs Willis

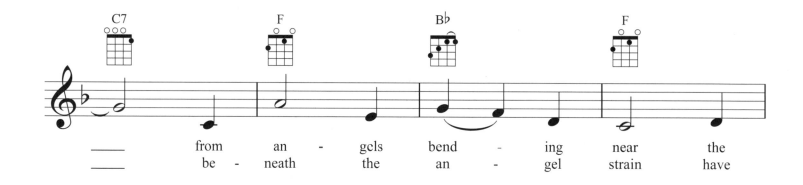

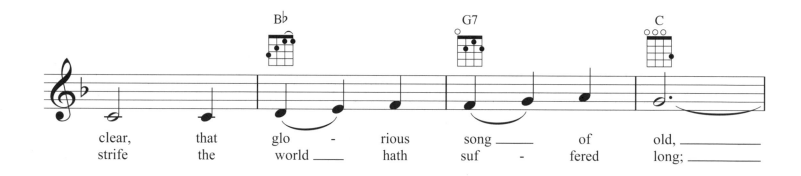

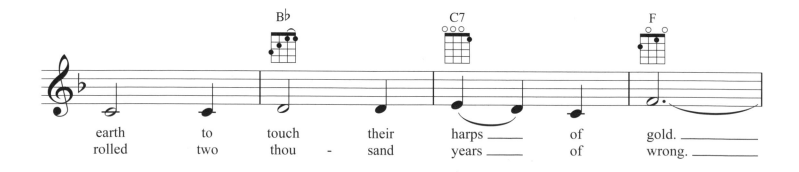

Additional Lyrics

3. And ye, beneath life's crushing load,
   Whose forms are bending low,
   Who toil along the climbing way
   With painful steps and slow;
   Look now, for glad and golden hours
   Come swiftly on the wing.
   O rest beside the weary road
   And hear the angels sing.

4. For lo, the days are hast'ning on,
   By prophet bards foretold,
   When with the ever-circling years
   Comes round the age of gold;
   When peace shall over all the earth
   Its ancient splendors fling,
   And the whole world give back the song
   Which now the angels sing.

It's Beginning to Look Like Christmas

By Meredith Willson

It's Christmas in New York

Words and Music by William Butt

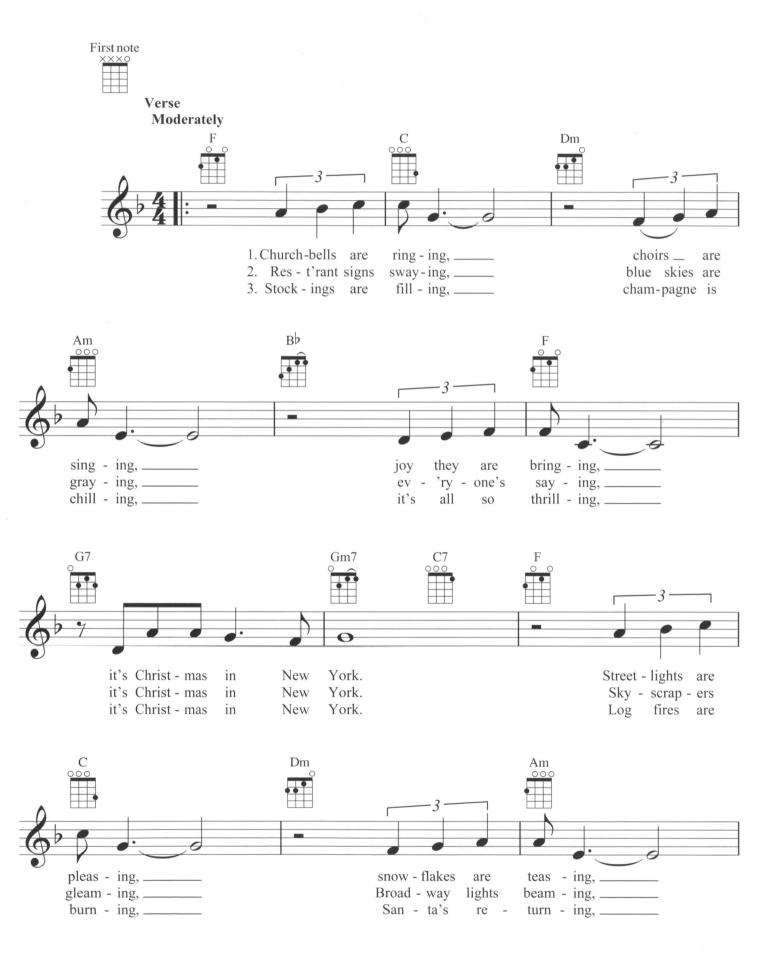

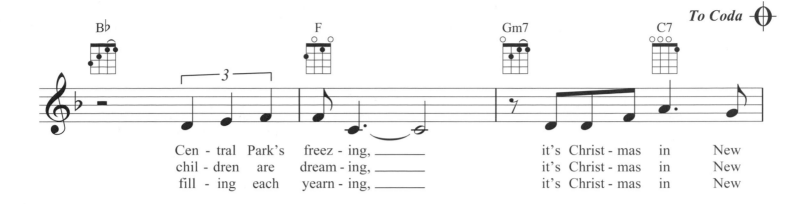

Cen - tral Park's freez - ing, _____ it's Christ - mas in New
chil - dren are dream - ing, _____ it's Christ - mas in New
fill - ing each yearn - ing, _____ it's Christ - mas in New

Bridge

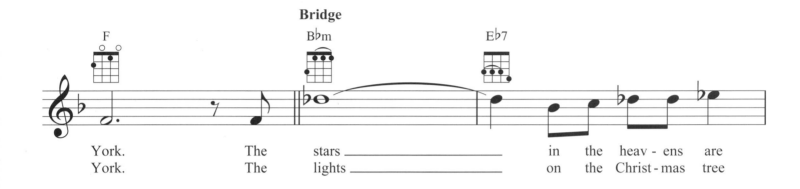

York. The stars _____ in the heav - ens are
York. The lights _____ on the Christ - mas tree

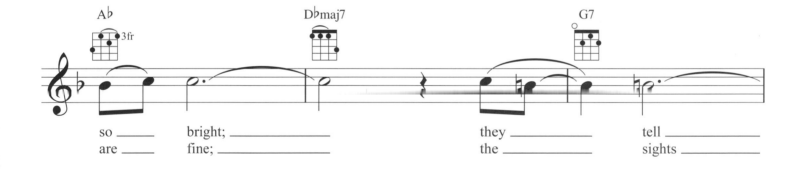

so _____ bright; _____ they _____ tell _____
are _____ fine; _____ the _____ sights _____

2nd time, D.C. al Coda

____ of a ba - by that was born _____ on this night.
____ of the shop - ping sprees, the gifts, _____ yours and mine.

Joy to the World
(A Christmas Prayer)

Words and Music by Kevin Jonas, Sr. and Nicholas Jonas

Lord, we find __ their end - ing as we take an - oth - er view. __ My

hope is that __ this Christ - mas prayer __ would some - how __ come true.

⊕ **Coda**

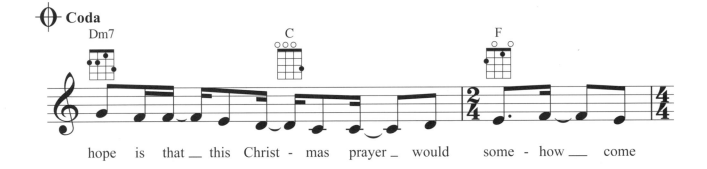

hope is that __ this Christ - mas prayer __ would some - how __ come

Outro

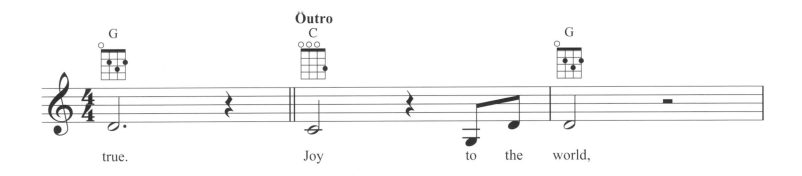

true. Joy to the world,

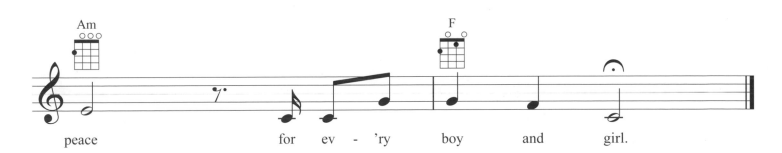

peace for ev - 'ry boy and girl.

Jesus Born on This Day

Words and Music by Mariah Carey and Walter Afanasieff

born on this day, ____ 1., 3. He is our light ____ and sal - va -
2. Heav - en - ly Child ____ in a man -

- tion. ____ Oh, Je - sus, ____
- ger. ____ Oh, Je - sus, ____

born on this day, ____ He is the King ____ of all na -
born on this day, ____ He is our Lord ____ and our Sav -

1., 2.   3.

- tions. ____   - tions. ____
- ior. ____

Outro-Verse

To - day a Child is ___ born on earth. (To - day a

Outro

Lo, How a Rose E'er Blooming

15th Century German Carol
Translated by Theodore Baker
Music from *Alte Catholische Geistliche Kirchengesang*

1. Lo, how a rose e'er bloom - ing, from ten - der stem hath sprung! Of Jes - se's lin - eage com - ing, as men of old have sung. It came, a flow'r - et bright, a - mid the cold of win - ter, when half - spent was the night.

2. I - sa - iah 'twas fore - told it, from the Rose I have in mind. With Mar - y we be - hold it, as the vir - gin moth - er kind. To show God's love a - right, she bore to men a Sav - ior, when half - spent was the night.

Joseph's Lullaby

Words and Music by Bart Millard and Brown Bannister

Fa - ther guard Your heart for now so You can ___ sleep to my -
ask that He, for just this mo - ment, sim - ply ___ be my ___

1.
\- night?

2.
___ child.

Verse
3. Go to sleep, my ___

___ son. Ba - by, close Your eyes. _____

Soon e - nough You'll save the day, ___ but for now, dear child of ___

___ mine, _____ oh, my _____ Je -

sus, sleep tight.

* Let chord ring.

125

The Little Drummer Boy

Words and Music by Harry Simeone, Henry Onorati and Katherine Davis

	C	C7	F
to	lay	be -	fore	the	King,	pa	rum	pum	pum	pum,
that's	fit	to	give	our	King,	pa	rum	pum	pum	pum,
I	played	my	best	for	Him,	pa	rum	pum	pum	pum,

	C		G
rum	pum	pum	pum,	rum	pum	pum	pum, _____
rum	pum	pum	pum,	rum	pum	pum	pum. _____
rum	pum	pum	pum,	rum	pum	pum	pum. _____

C		G7sus4	C
so	to	hon - or	Him,	pa	rum	pum	pum	pum, _____
Shall	I	play	for	you,	pa	rum	pum	pum	pum, _____
Then	He	smiled	at	me,	pa	rum	pum	pum	pum, _____

	G7	C
____		
____	when ___ we	come. _____
____	on _____ my	drum? _____
____	me and my	drum. _____

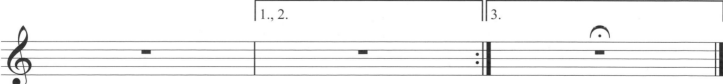

1., 2.   3.

A Marshmallow World

Words by Carl Sigman
Music by Peter De Rose

First note

Verse
Moderately bright, in 2

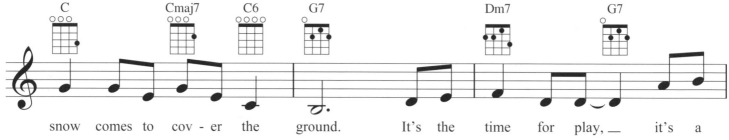

It's a marsh - mal - low world in the win - ter _____ when the

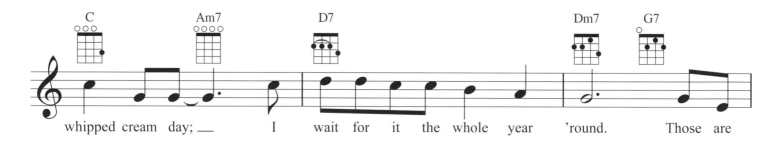

snow comes to cov - er the ground. It's the time for play, _ it's a

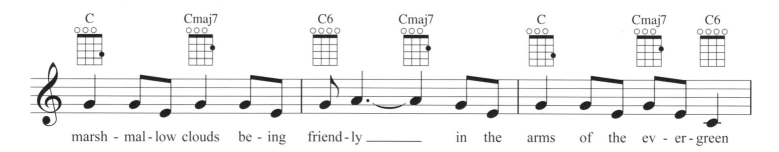

whipped cream day; _ I wait for it the whole year 'round. Those are

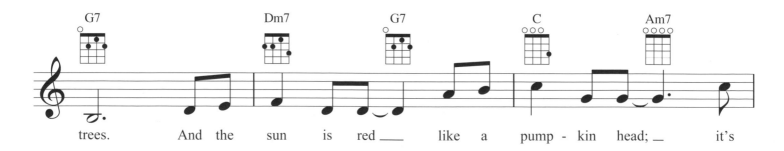

marsh - mal - low clouds be - ing friend - ly _____ in the arms of the ev - er - green

trees. And the sun is red _ like a pump - kin head; _ it's

Bridge

shin - ing so your nose won't freeze. The world is your snow - ball;

see how it grows. That's how it goes when - ev - er it snows. The

world is your snow - ball just for a song; get out and roll it a -

Outro-Verse

long. It's a yum - yum - my world made for sweet - hearts; _____ take a

walk with your fa - vor - ite girl. It's a sug - ar date; _ what if

spring is late? _ In win - ter it's a marsh - mal - low world.

Mary, Did You Know?

Words and Music by Mark Lowry and Buddy Greene

First note

Moderately

Verse

Am · · · G

1. Mar - y, did you know that your ba - by boy ___ would
(2.) know that your ba - by boy ___ will
(3.) know that your ba - by boy ___ is

Dm · · · E7sus4 · E7 · Am

one day walk ___ on wa - ter? Mar - y, did you know that your ba -
give sight to ___ a blind ___ man? Mar - y, did you know that your ba -
Lord of all ___ cre - a - tion? Mar - y, did you know that your ba -

G · · · Dm · · · E7sus4 · E7

- by boy ___ would save our sons ___ and daugh - ters? Did you know ___
- by boy ___ would calm a storm ___ with His ___ hand? Did you know ___
- by boy ___ will one day rule ___ the na - tions? Did you know ___

Dm · · · G · · · C · G

___ that your ba - by boy ___ has come to make ___ you new? ___
___ that your ba - by boy ___ has walked where an - gels trod, ___
___ that your ba - by boy ___ was heav - en's per - fect Lamb, ___

Am · · · Dm

To Coda ⊕

___ This child ___ that you ___ de - liv - ered will
___ and when you kiss your lit - tle ba - by, you've
___ and the sleep - ing child ___ you're hold -

Most of All I Wish You Were Here

Music and Lyrics by Denise Osso

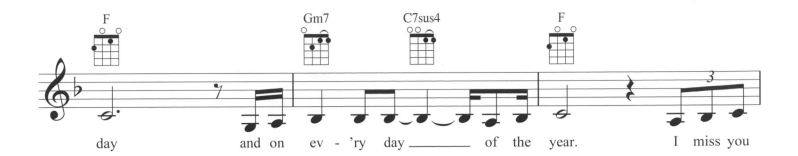

day   and on ev - 'ry day _____ of the year.   I miss you

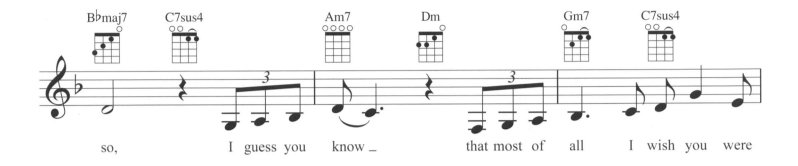

so,   I guess you know _ that most of all   I wish you were

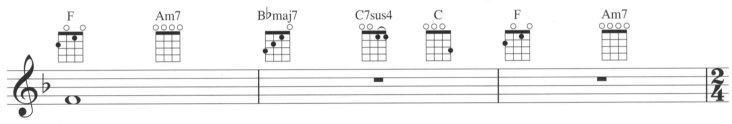

here.

Verse

2. I've   sent my cards and trimmed the tree,

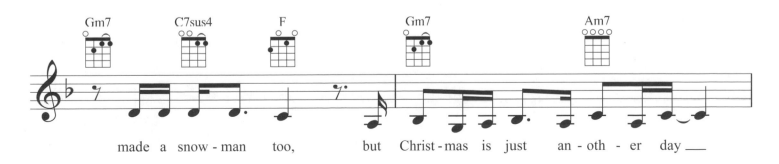

made a snow - man too,   but Christ - mas is just an - oth - er day _____

when I'm not ___ with you.   I pray we'll be to - geth - er a - gain

just like we used to be.   I send you my love; you can keep it 'til then,

Pre-Chorus

when you come home to me. ___   Mer - ry Christ - mas, O my dear.   God

keep you safe from harm.   When you come home I'll still be

here   to hold you in my arms. ___   I wish you

The Most Wonderful Time of the Year

Words and Music by Eddie Pola and George Wyle

2.

hap - hap-pi-est sea - son of all. _____

Bridge

_____ There'll be par - ties for host-ing, marsh -

mal - lows for toast - ing and car - ol - ing out in the snow.

There'll be scar - y ghost sto - ries and tales of the glo - ries of

D.S. al Coda

Christ - mas - es long, long a - go. _____ 3. It's the

Coda

most won - der - ful time _____ of the

year. _____

Noel

Words and Music by Matt Redman, Chris Tomlin and Ed Cash

1. Love in-car-nate, love di-vine.
2. Son of God and Son of Man,

Star and an-gels gave the sign.
there be-fore the world be-gan.

Bow to Babe on bend-ed knee,
Born to suf-fer, born to save,

the Sav-ior of hu-man-i-ty.
born to raise us from the grave.

Un-to us a Child is born.
Christ, the ev-er-last-ing Lord,

He shall reign for-ev-er-more.
He shall reign for-ev-er-more.

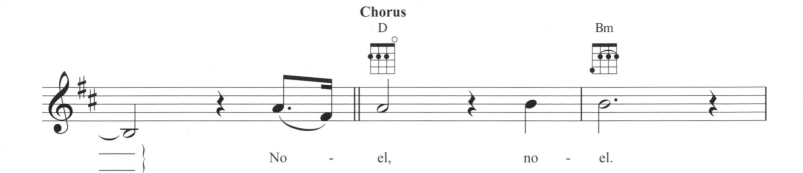

Chorus

No - el, no - el.

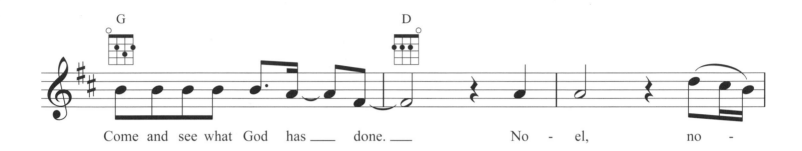

Come and see what God has ___ done. ___ No - el, no -

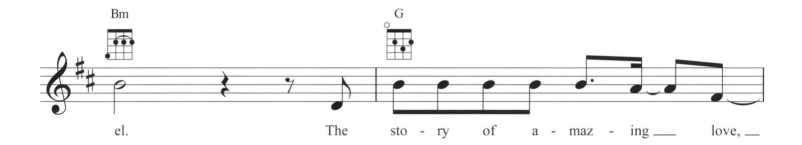

el. The sto - ry of a - maz - ing ___ love, ___

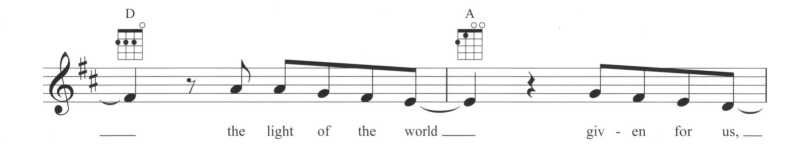

___ the light of the world ___ giv - en for us, ___

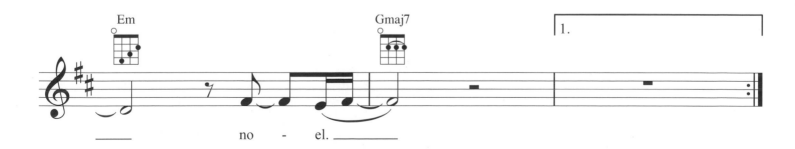

___ no - el. _____

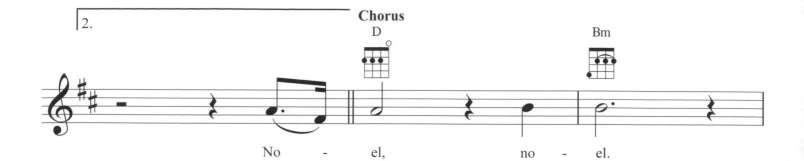

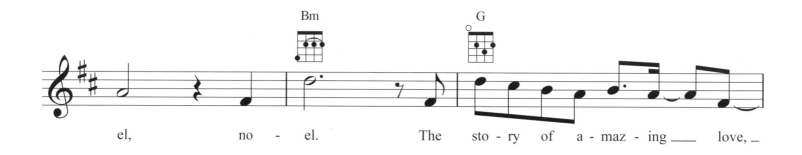

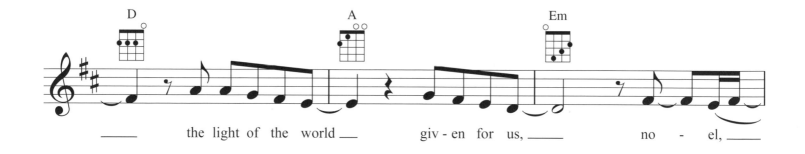

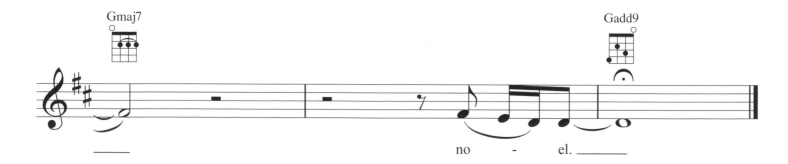

Merry Christmas, Darling

Words and Music by Richard Carpenter and Frank Pooler

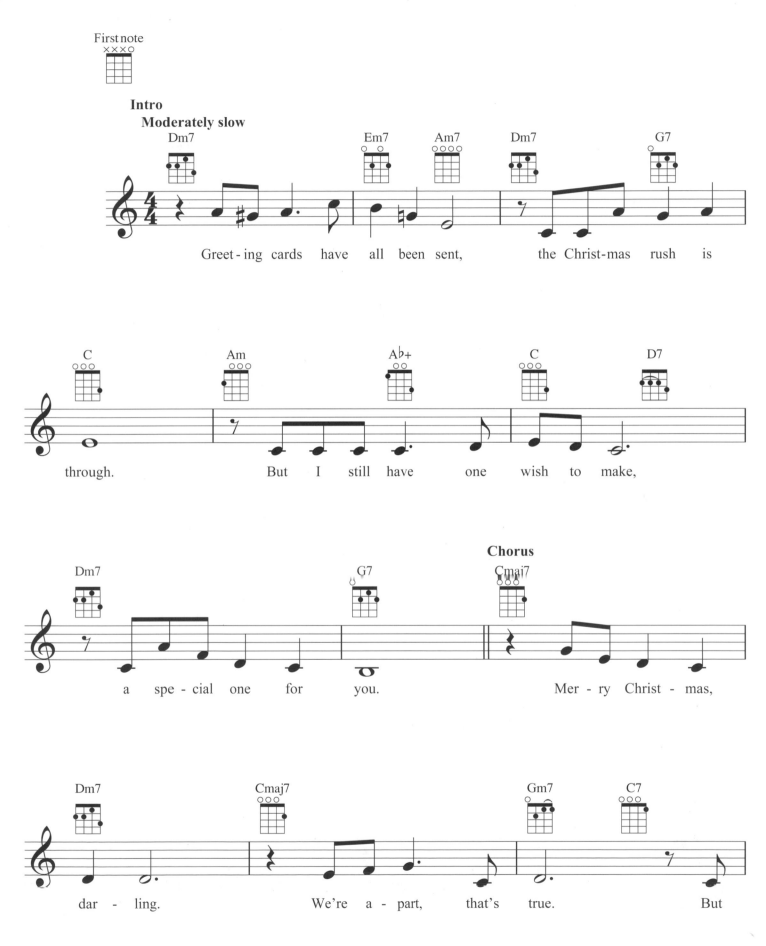

I can dream, and in my dreams, I'm Christ - mas - ing with

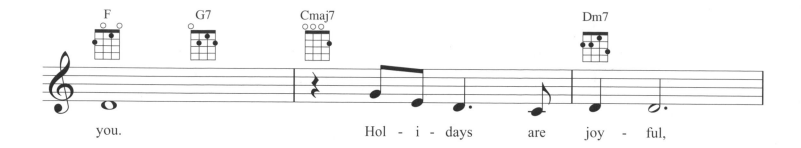

you. Hol - i - days are joy - ful,

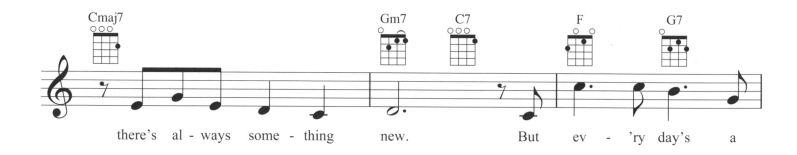

there's al - ways some - thing new. But ev - 'ry day's a

hol - i - day when I'm near to you. The ___

lights on my tree I wish you could see, I wish it ev - 'ry

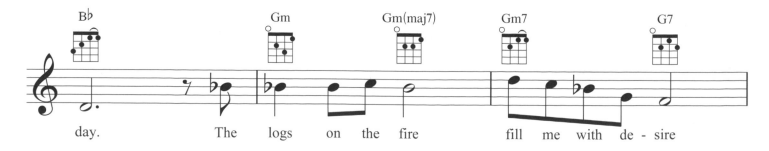

day. The logs on the fire fill me with de - sire

to see you and to _____ say that I

Outro-Chorus

wish you Mer - ry Christ - mas, Hap - py New Year,

too. I've just one wish on this Christ - mas Eve:

D.S. al Coda

I wish I were with you. The ____

Coda

I wish I were with you.

I wish I were with you. _____

Not That Far from Bethlehem

Words and Music by Jeff Borders, Gayla Borders and Lowell Alexander

1. Un-der-neath _ the stars, ___ just a sim-ple man and
2. Let us cel-e-brate ___ as the Christ-mas-es go

wife. Some-where in ___ the dark, ___ his words cut the si-lent
by, learn to live ___ our days ___ with our hearts near to the

night: "Take my hand, for the child that you car-ry is God's
Child, ev-er drawn, ev-er close to the on-ly love that

own. ___ And though it seems the ___
lasts. ___ And though two thou-sand ___

Chorus

road is long, ___ } we're not that far ___ from
years have passed, __ }

145

O Christmas Tree

Traditional German Carol

Miss You Most at Christmas Time

Words and Music by Mariah Carey and Walter Afanasieff

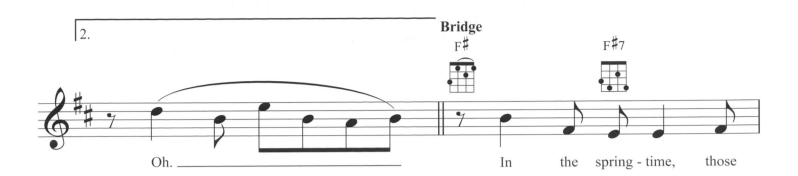

Bridge

Oh. _____ In the spring - time, those

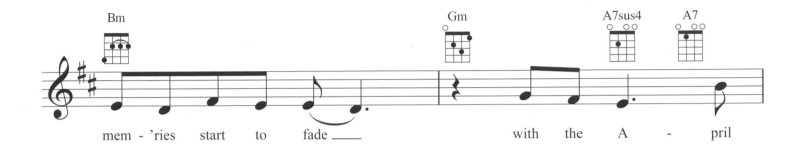

mem - 'ries start to fade _____ with the A - pril

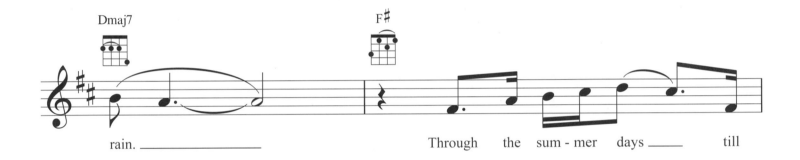

rain. _____ Through the sum - mer days _____ till

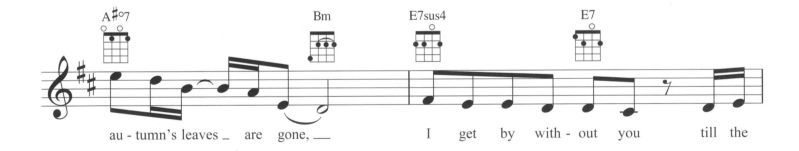

au - tumn's leaves _ are gone, _____ I get by with - out you till the

D.S. al Coda

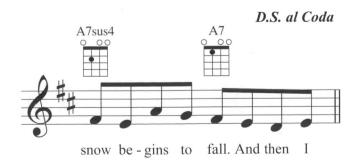

snow be - gins to fall. And then I

Coda

time. _____

O Come, All Ye Faithful

Music by John Francis Wade
Latin Words translated by Frederick Oakeley

O Come, O Come, Emmanuel

Traditional Latin Text
V. 1, 2 translated by John M. Neale
V. 3 translated by Henry S. Coffin
15th Century French Melody
Adapted by Thomas Helmore

O Holy Night

French Words by Placide Cappeau
English Words by John S. Dwight
Music by Adolphe Adam

1. O ho-ly night the stars are bright-ly shin-
2. Tru-ly He taught us to love one an-oth-

ing; it is the night of the dear Sav-ior's birth.
er. His law is love, and His gos-pel is peace.

Long lay the world in sin and er-ror pin-
Chains shall He break, for the slave is our broth-

ing, 'til He ap-peared and the soul felt its worth. A
er, and in His name all op-pres-sion shall cease. Sweet

thrill of hope the wea-ry world re-joic-es, for
hymns of joy in grate-ful cho-rus raise we. Let

yon - der breaks a new and glo - rious morn. Fall _____ on your
all with - in us praise His ho - ly name. Christ _____ is the

knees, _____ O hear _____ the an - gel voic - es! O
Lord, _____ O praise _____ His name for - ev - er! His

night _____ di - vine! _____ O _____ night _____ when Christ was
pow'r _____ and glo - ry _____ ev - er - more pro-

1.
born! _____ O night! _____ O ho - ly
claim! _____ His

2.
night! O night di - vine! _____ pow'r _____ and glo -

- ry _____ ev - er - more pro - claim. _____

O Little Town of Bethlehem

Words by Phillips Brooks
Music by Lewis H. Redner

1. O lit - tle town of Beth - le - hem, how still we __ see thee
2. For Christ is born of Mar - y, and gath - ered __ all a -
3. O ho - ly Child of Beth - le - hem, de - scend to __ us, we

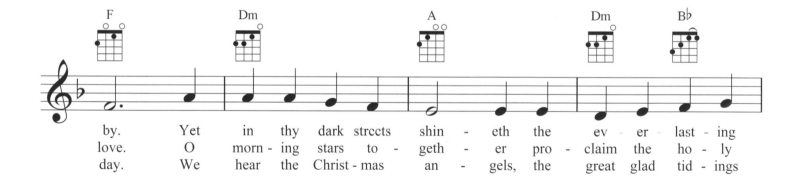

lie! A - bove thy deep and dream - less sleep, the si - lent __ stars go
bove, while mor - tals sleep, the an - gels keep their watch of __ won - d'ring
pray. Cast out our sin and en - ter in, be born in __ us to -

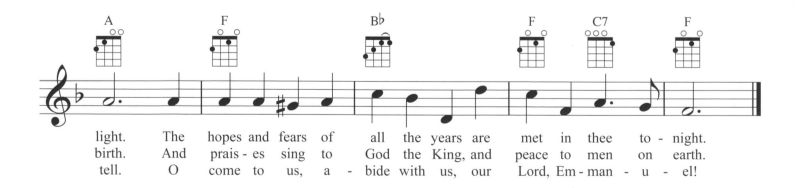

by. Yet in thy dark streets shin - eth the ev - er - last - ing
love. O morn - ing stars to - geth - er pro - claim the ho - ly
day. We hear the Christ - mas an - gels, the great glad tid - ings

light. The hopes and fears of all the years are met in thee to - night.
birth. And prais - es sing to God the King, and peace to men on earth.
tell. O come to us, a - bide with us, our Lord, Em - man - u - el!

An Old Fashioned Christmas

Words and Music by Richard Carpenter and John Bettis

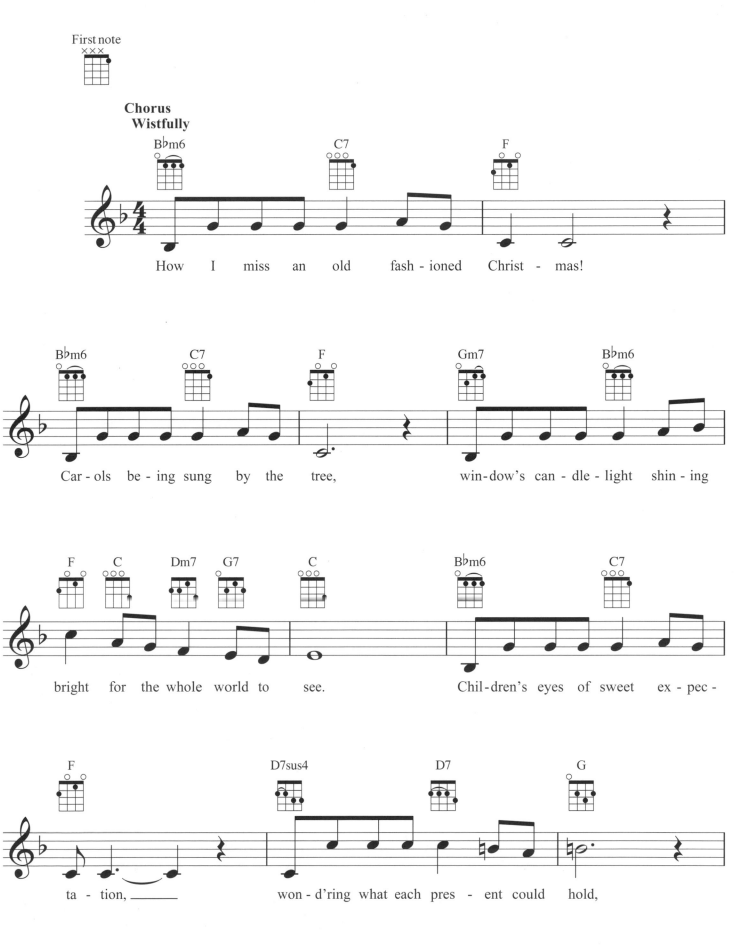

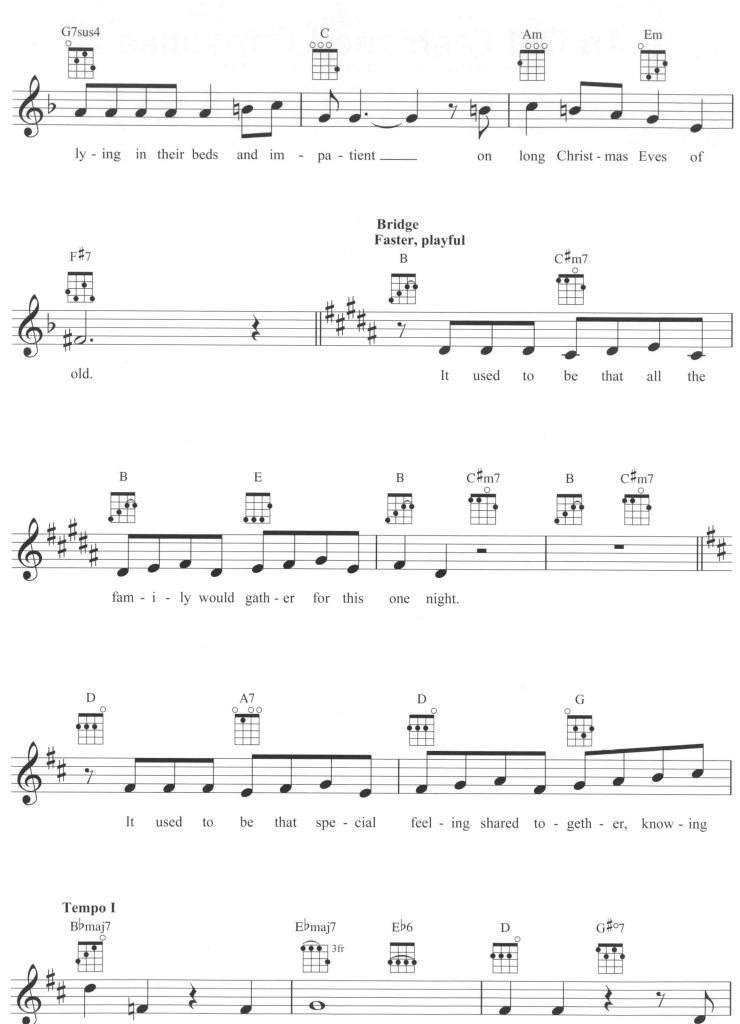

ly - ing   in their beds   and im - pa - tient _____   on   long Christ - mas Eves of

Bridge
Faster, playful

old.   It   used   to   be   that   all   the

fam - i - ly would gath - er   for   this   one   night.

It   used   to   be   that spe - cial   feel - ing shared to - geth - er, know - ing

Tempo I

Christ - mas   was   here   one   night   a

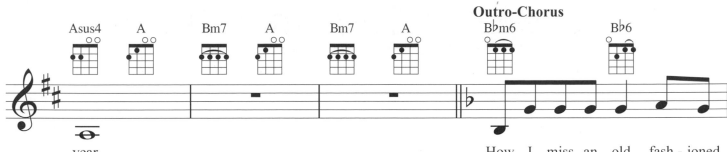

Outro-Chorus

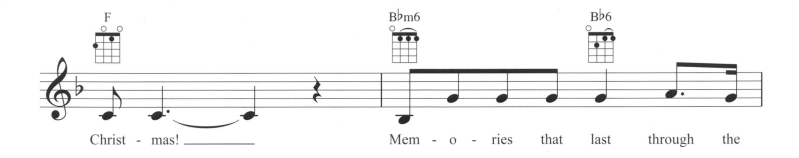

year.

How I miss an old fash - ioned

Christ - mas! _____ Mem - o - ries that last through the

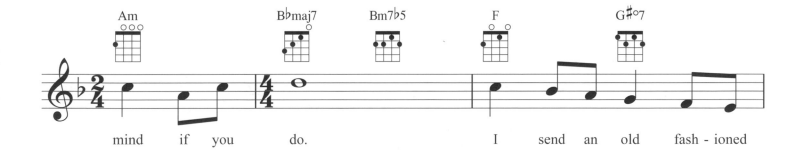

years. Call me sen - ti - men - tal; don't

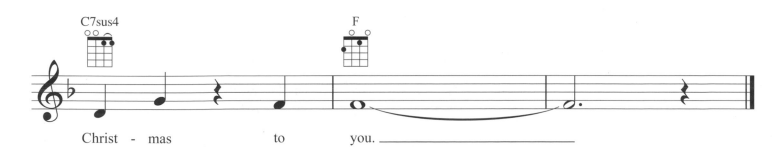

mind if you do. I send an old fash - ioned

Christ - mas to you. _____

One Little Christmas Tree

Words and Music by Ronald N. Miller and Bryan Wells

Em   B+   G   C#m7♭5

I'm so a - fraid and so a - lone.   Could
a voice that was heard through - out the world.   "Go

F   C   Dm   F

one lit - tle Christ - mas tree, so ti - ny and small
down, lit - tle an - gel girl, and give him your star. To -

Dm7   **Chorus**   G7   C

light up some - one's home?" — 'Cause — one lit - tle Christ - mas tree can
night he'll light the world." — 'Cause — one lit - tle Christ - mas tree can

Am   C   Dm   G7

light up a home so one lit - tle child can find a toy.
light up the world so those who are lost may find their way.

Dm   A+   F   G7

One lit - tle Christ - mas tree can light up a home so
One lit - tle Christ - mas tree can light up the world so

Dm7   G7   1. C   2. C

one lit - tle heart — can find some joy.
all men — may see on Christ - mas   Day.

Precious Promise

Words and Music by Steven Curtis Chapman

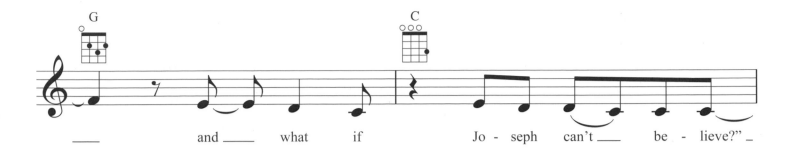

_____ and _____ what if Jo - seph can't _____ be - lieve?" _

_____ And her ques - tions and _____ her fears _____ are

met with an o - ver-whelm - ing joy _____ that

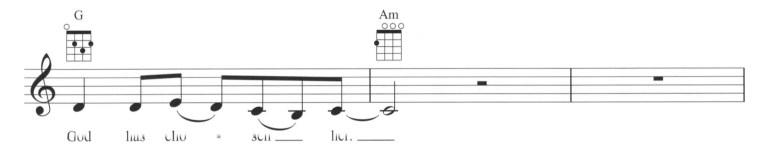

God has cho - sen _____ her. _____

To Coda ⊕

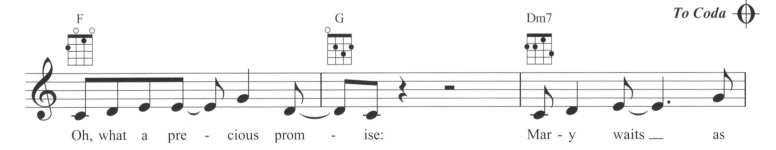

Oh, what a pre - cious prom - ise: Mar - y waits _____ as

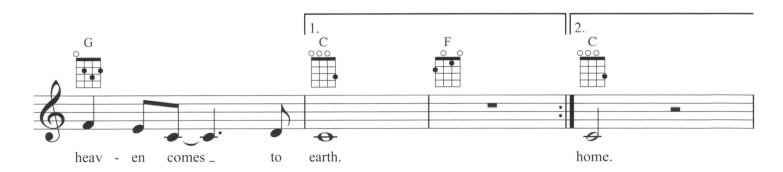

heav - en comes _ to earth. home.

Bridge

And shep - herds stand on a

hill - side, their hearts rac - ing with the news

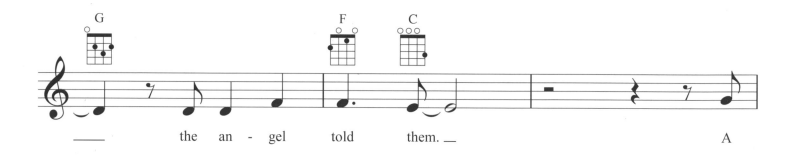

the an - gel told them. A

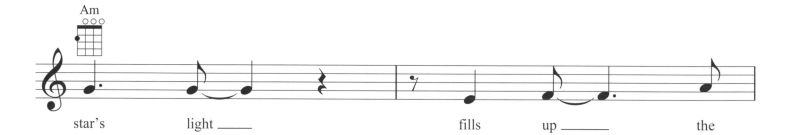

star's light fills up the

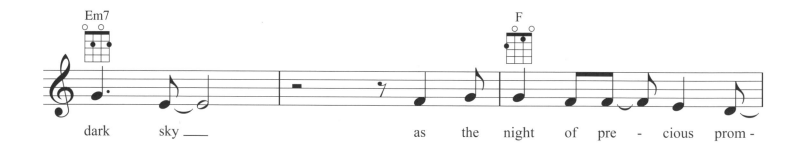

dark sky as the night of pre - cious prom -

D.S. al Coda

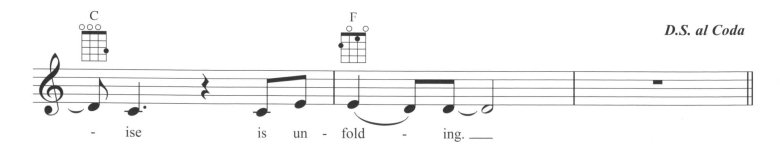

- ise is un - fold - ing.

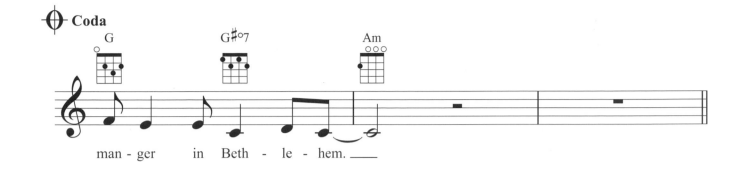

Coda

man - ger   in   Beth - le - hem. ____

Outro

Oh, what a pre - cious prom - ise,   ly - ing in ____   a

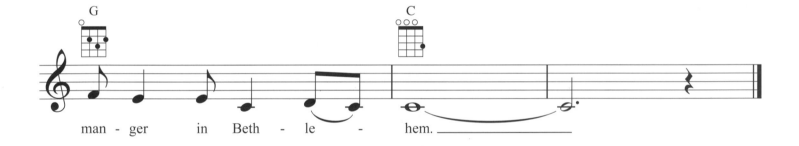

man - ger   in   Beth - le - hem. ____

Additional Lyrics

3. Oh, what a precious promise. Oh, what a gift of love.
   Joseph makes his choice to do what few men would have done:
   To take Mary as his bride when she's already carrying a child that isn't his own.
   Oh, what a precious promise: Mary and the child will have a home.

4. Oh, what a precious promise. Oh, what a gift of love.
   The waiting now is over and the time has finally come
   For the God who made this world to roll back the curtain and
      unveil His passion for the heart of man.
   Oh, what a precious promise, lying in a manger in Bethlehem.

Pretty Paper

Words and Music by Willie Nelson

First note

Verse
Flowing

Crowd - ed streets, bus - y feet hus - tle

by him. _____ Down - town shop - pers, Christ - mas is

nigh. _____ There he sits all a - lone on the

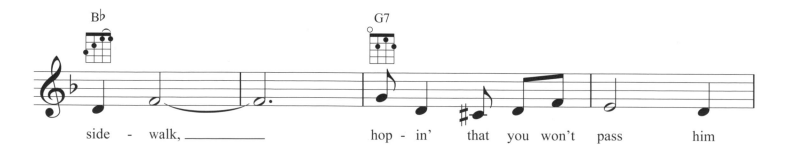

side - walk, _____ hop - in' that you won't pass him

by. _____ Should you stop? Bet - ter not; much too

bus - y. _____ You'd bet - ter hur - ry; my,

how time does fly! _____ And in the

dis - tance the ring - ing of ____ laugh - ter, _____

____ and in the midst of the laugh - ter he

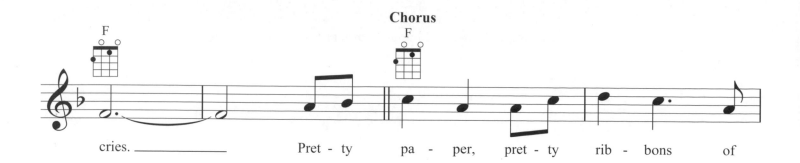

Chorus

cries. _____ Pret - ty pa - per, pret - ty rib - bons of

blue, _____ wrap your pres - ents to your dar - ling from

you. _____ Pret - ty pen - cils to write, "I love

you." _____ Oh, pret - ty pa - per, pret - ty

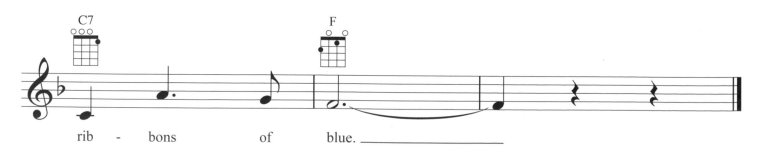

rib - bons of blue. _____

Please Come Home for Christmas

Words and Music by Charles Brown and Gene Redd

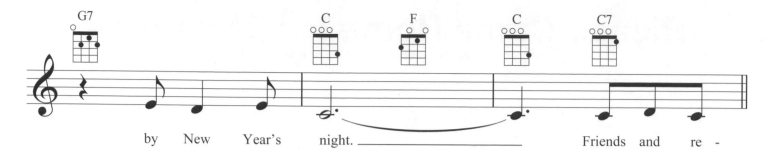

by New Year's night. _____ Friends and re -

Bridge

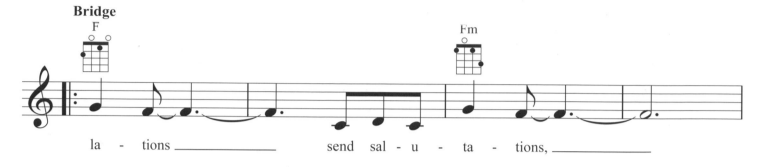

la - tions _____ send sal - u - ta - tions, _____

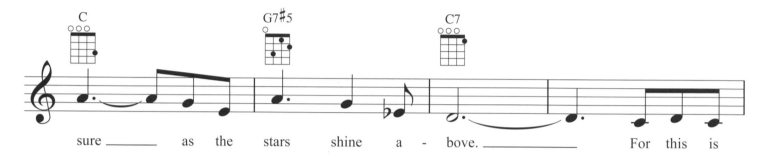

sure _____ as the stars shine a - bove. _____ For this is

Christ - mas, _____ yes, Christ - mas, my dear. _____

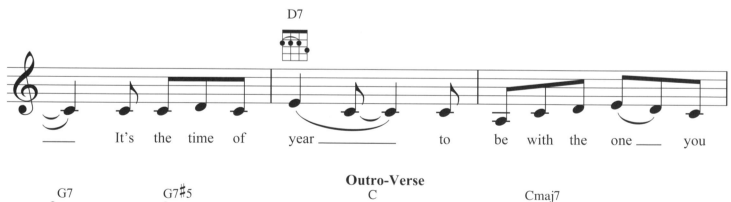

_____ It's the time of year _____ to be with the one ___ you

Outro-Verse

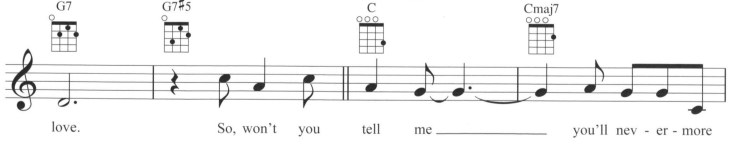

love. So, won't you tell me _____ you'll nev - er - more

roam? _____ Christ - mas and New Year _____

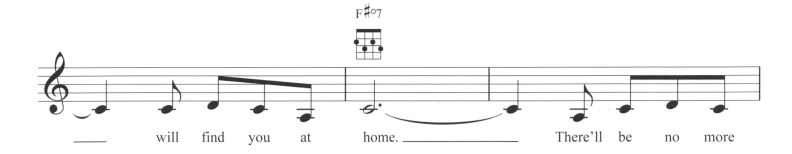

_____ will find you at home. _____ There'll be no more

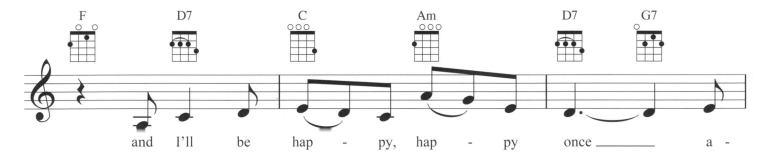

sor - row, ___ no grief ___ and pain, _____

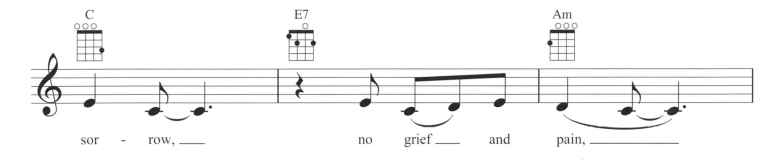

and I'll be hap - py, hap - py once _____ a -

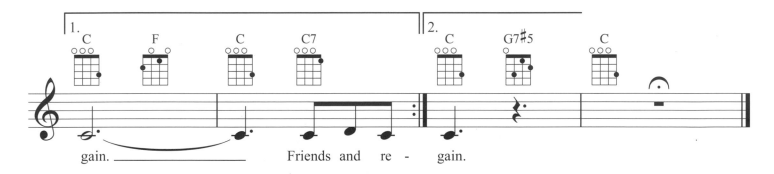

gain. _____ Friends and re - gain.

Additional Lyrics

2. Choirs will be singing "Silent Night,"
   Christmas carols by candlelight.
   Please come home for Christmas,
   Please come home for Christmas.
   If not for Christmas, by New Year's night.

River

Words and Music by Joni Mitchell

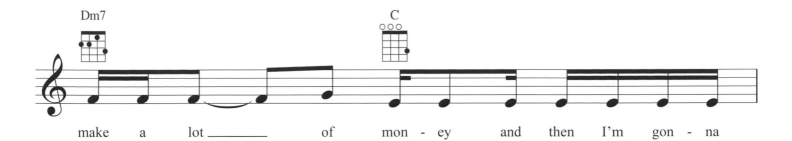

make a lot _____ of mon - ey and then I'm gon - na

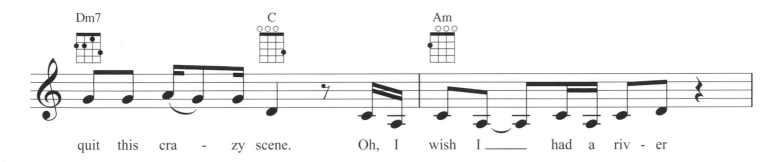

quit this cra - zy scene. Oh, I wish I _____ had a riv - er

I could skate _____ a - way ___ on.   I

Chorus

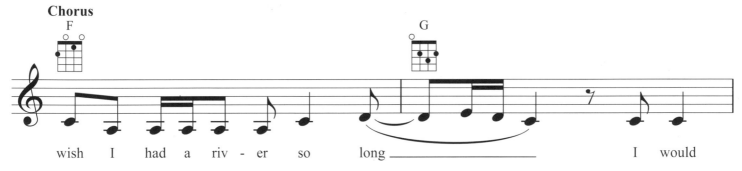

wish I had a riv - er so long _____ I would

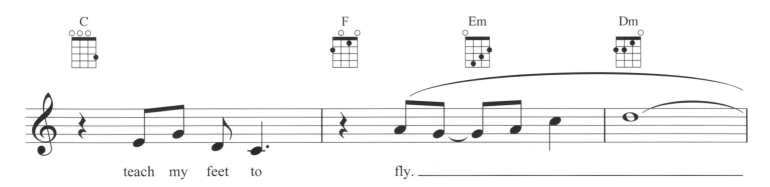

teach my feet to   fly. _____

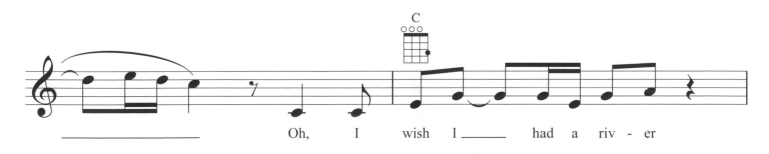

_____   Oh, I wish I _____ had a riv - er

Additional Lyrics

2. He tried hard to help me, you know, he put me at ease.
   He loved me so naughty, made me weak in the knees.
   Oh, I wish I had a river I could skate away on.
   I'm so hard to handle, I'm selfish and I'm sad.
   Now I've gone and lost the best baby that I ever had.
   Oh, I wish I had a river I could skate away on.

Silent Night

Words by Joseph Mohr
Translated by John F. Young
Music by Franz X. Gruber

Silver and Gold

Music and Lyrics by Johnny Marks

Chorus
Slowly and expressively

Sil - ver and gold, sil - ver and gold,

ev - 'ry - one wish - es for sil - ver and gold.

How do you meas - ure its worth? _____

Just by the pleas - ure it gives here on earth.

Sil - ver and gold, sil - ver and gold mean so much more when I see ____ sil - ver and gold dec - o - ra - tions ____ on ev - 'ry Christ - mas

1. tree.

2. tree. ____

Silver Bells

from the Paramount Picture THE LEMON DROP KID
Words and Music by Jay Livingston and Ray Evans

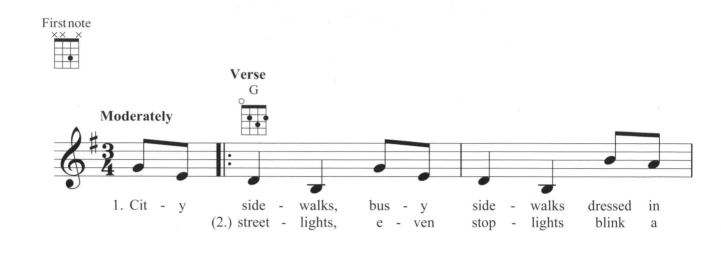

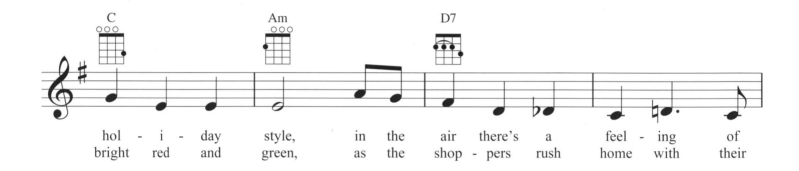

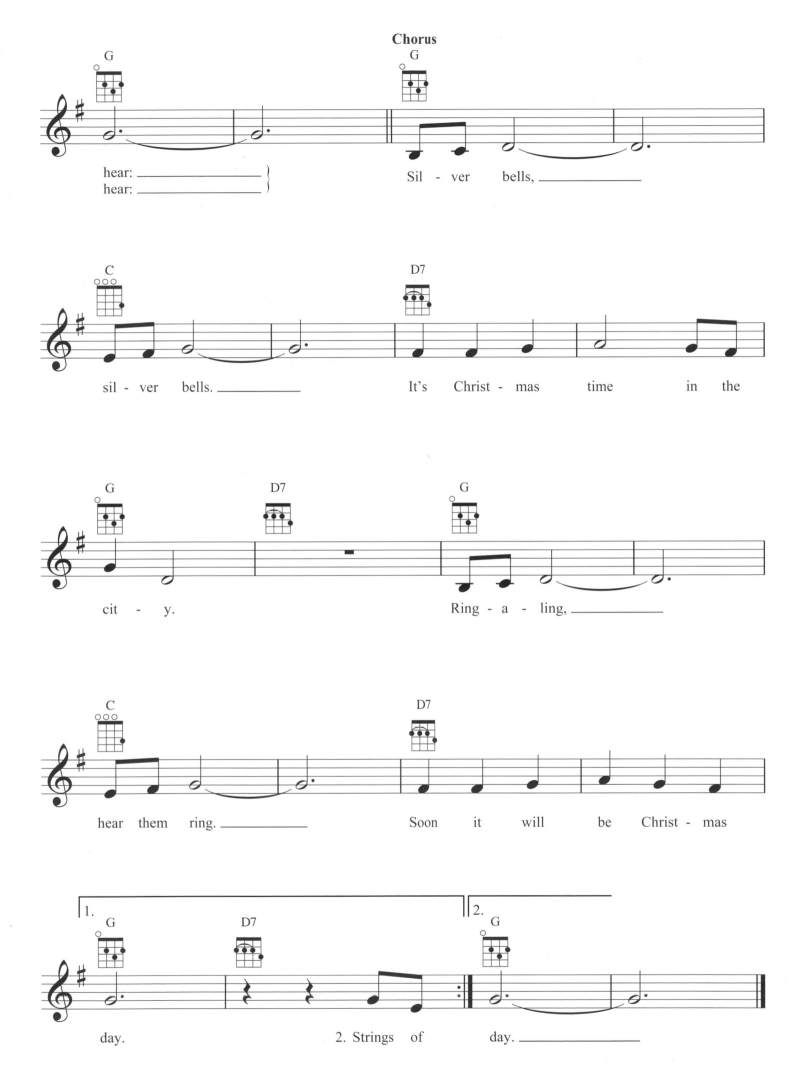

Snowfall

Lyrics by Ruth Thornhill
Music by Claude Thornhill

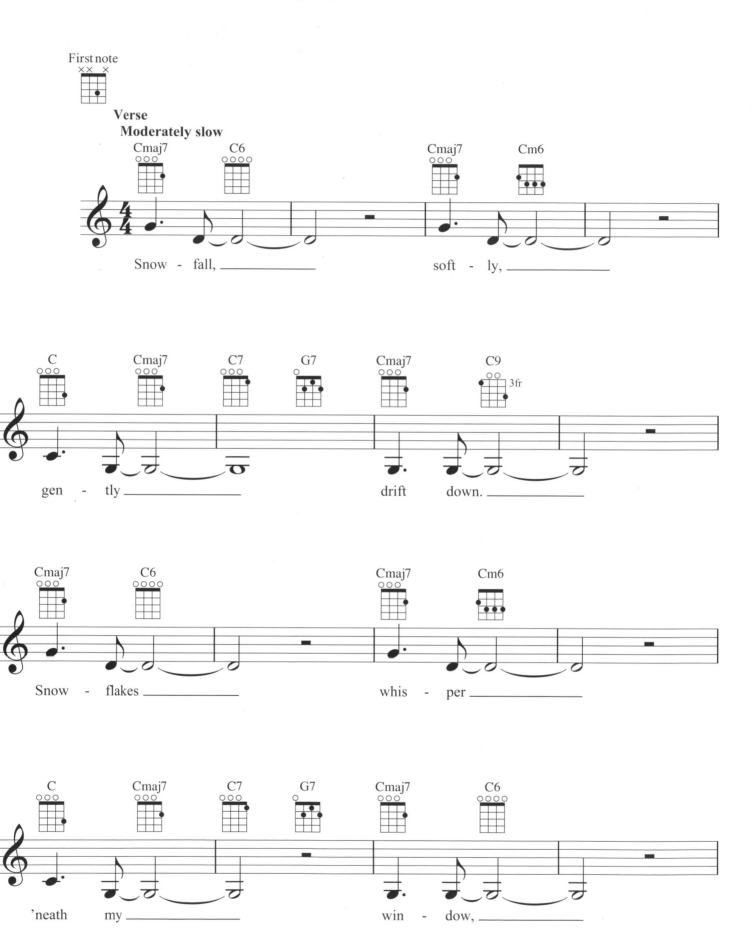

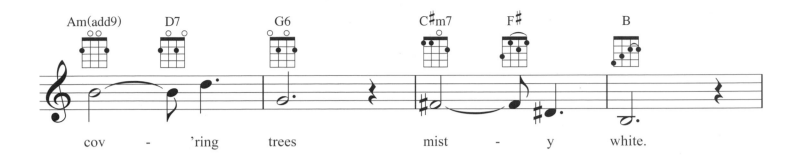

cov - 'ring trees   mist - y   white.

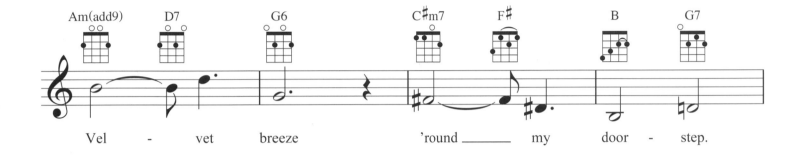

Vel - vet   breeze   'round _____ my   door - step.

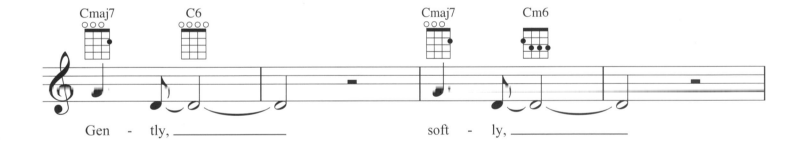

Gen - tly, _____   soft - ly, _____

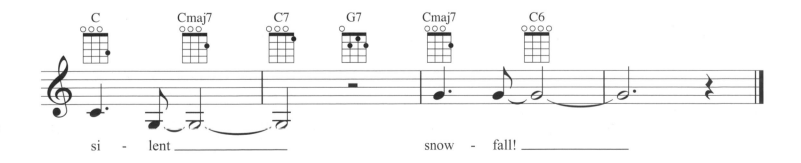

si - lent _____   snow - fall! _____

Some Children See Him

Lyric by Wihla Hutson
Music by Alfred Burt

Somewhere in My Memory

from the Twentieth Century Fox Motion Picture HOME ALONE
Words by Leslie Bricusse
Music by John Williams

Star of Bethlehem

from the Twentieth Century Fox Motion Picture HOME ALONE
Words by Leslie Bricusse
Music by John Williams

Outro-Verse

Still, Still, Still

Salzburg Melody, c.1819
Traditional Austrian Text

1. Still, _____ still, _____ still, to _____ sleep is _____ now His _____
2. Sleep, _____ sleep, _____ sleep, while _____ we Thy _____ vig - il _____

will. On Mar - y's _____ breast He rests in _____ slum - ber,
keep. And an - gels _____ come from heav - en _____ sing - ing,

while we _____ pray in end - less _____ num - ber. Still, _____ still, _____
songs of _____ ju - bi - la - tion _____ bring - ing. Sleep, _____ sleep, _____

still, to _____ sleep is _____ now His _____ will.
sleep, while _____ we Thy _____ vig - il _____ keep.

Tennessee Christmas

Words and Music by Amy Grant and Gary Chapman

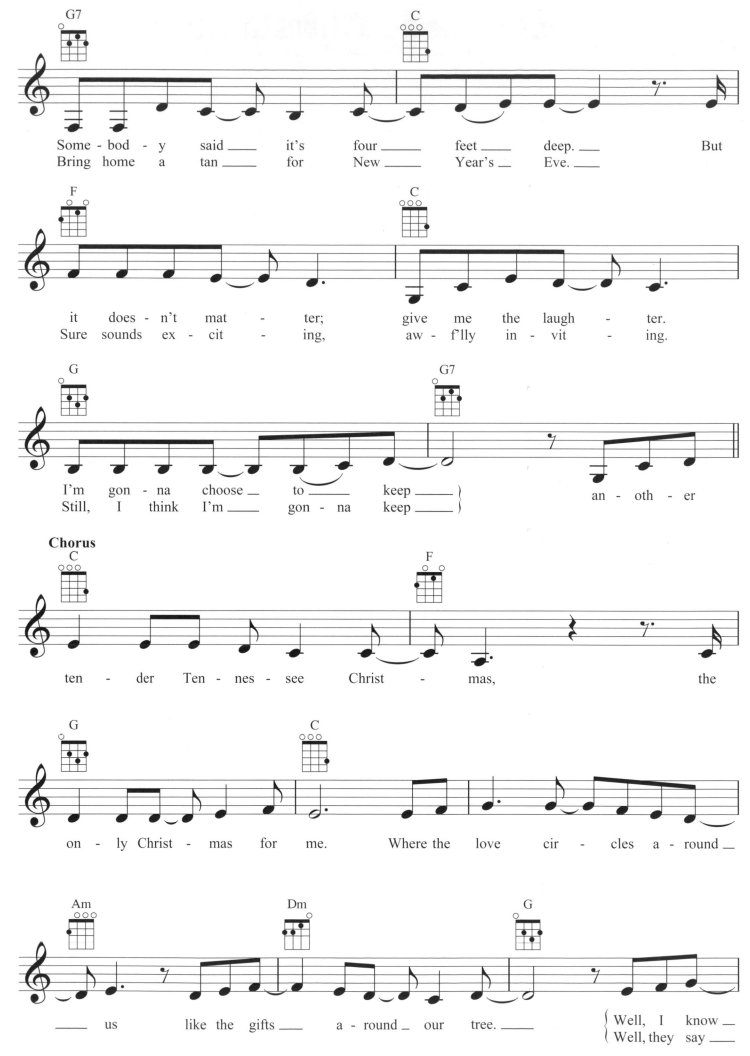

That Christmas Feeling

Words and Music by Bennie Benjamin and George David Weiss

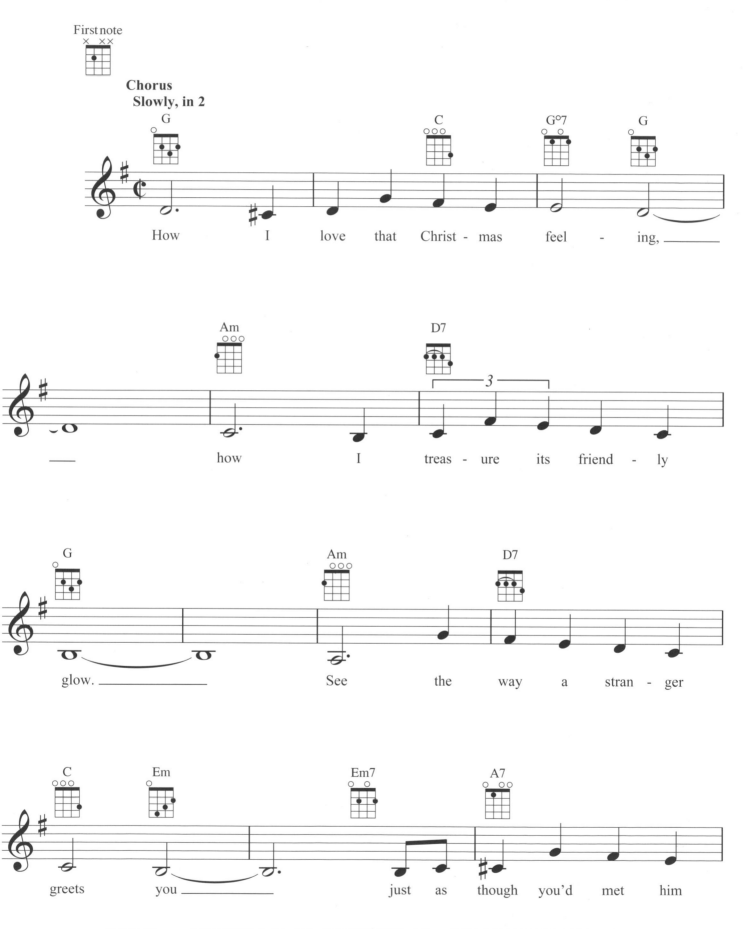

There's Still My Joy

Words and Music by Melissa Manchester, Matt Rollings and Beth Chapman

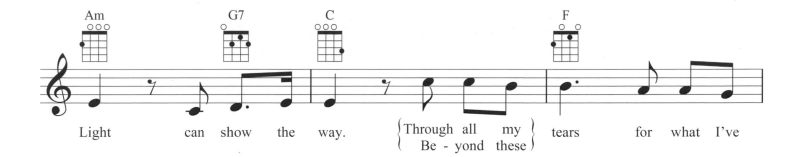

Light can show the way. {Through all my / Be - yond these} tears for what I've

To Coda ⊕

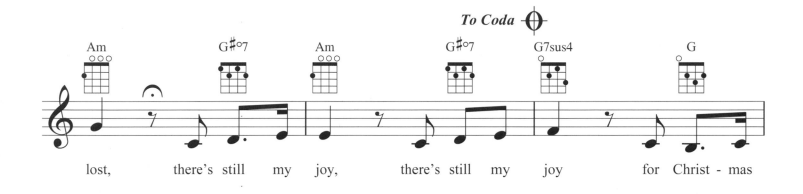

lost, there's still my joy, there's still my joy for Christ - mas

Day.

D.S. al Coda
(take 2nd ending)

3. The snow comes

⊕ **Coda**

joy for Christ - mas

Outro

Day. There's still my joy for Christ-mas Day.

191

2000 Decembers Ago

Words and Music by Joel Lindsey and Regie Hamm

thun - der? Did the moon find new rea - sons to
moun - tains till it filled up the val - leys be -
whelm - ing as it warmed ev - 'ry - one ___ in its

glow? ___ Could the chil - dren some - how ___ sense the
low? ___ Did all the world sense ___ love a -
flow, ___ for all of the earth ___ is still

won - der, two thou - sand De - cem - bers a - go? ___
bound - ing two thou - sand De - cem - bers a - go? ___
tell - ing of two thou - sand De - cem - bers a - go. ___

To Coda

1.
(Bum, bum, ___ bum, bah, bum, bum, ___ bum, bah.)

2. Were the

2.

Chorus

Was an - y - one a - ble to look ___

193

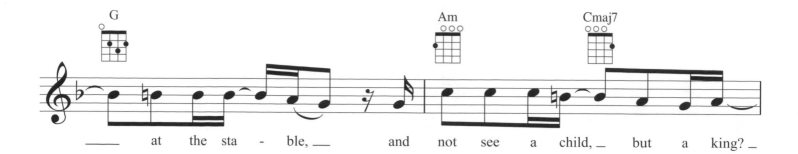

_____ at the sta - ble, _____ and not see a child, _ but a king? _

_____ I wish I could hear _ back o - ver the years _ as

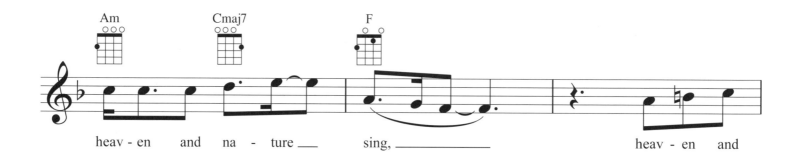

heav - en and na - ture _ sing, _____ heav - en and

na - ture _ sing. _____ Lo, _____ whoa. _____

(Bum, bum, _ bum, bah, bum, bum, _ bum, bah, bum, bum, _ bum, bah,

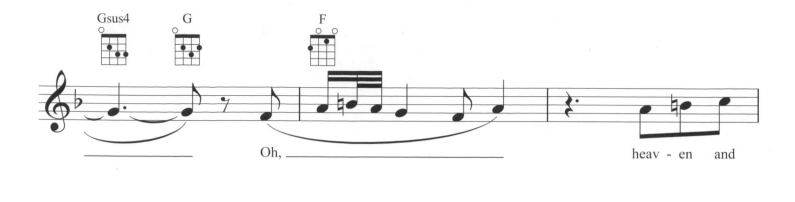

Oh, _____ heav - en and

na - ture ___ sing. _____ Lo, _____ whoa. ___

Outro

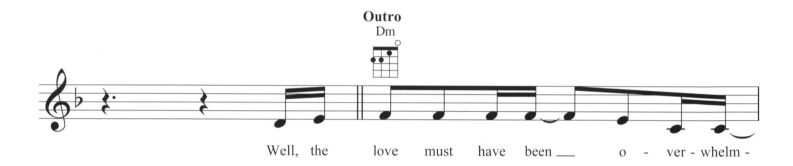

Well, the love must have been ___ o - ver - whelm -

- ing ___ two thou - sand De - cem - bers a - go. ___

(Bum, bum, ___ bum, bah,

bum, bum, ___ bum, bah, bum, bum, ___ bum, bah.)

Toyland

from BABES IN TOYLAND
Words by Glen MacDonough
Music by Victor Herbert

Ukrainian Bell Carol

Traditional
Music by Mykola Leontovych

First note

Joyfully

(Instrumental)

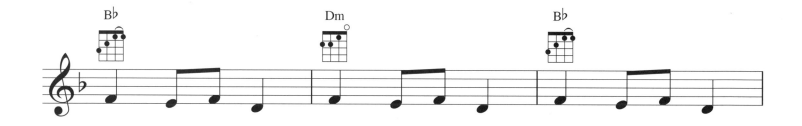

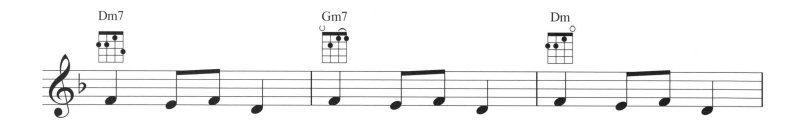

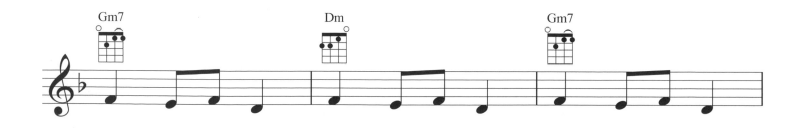

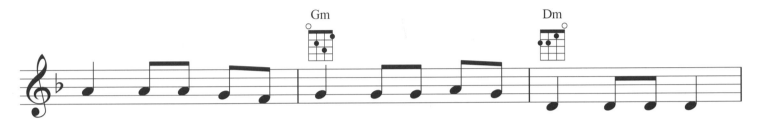

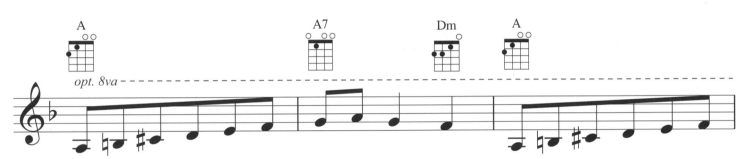

We Three Kings of Orient Are

Words and Music by John H. Hopkins, Jr.

Chorus

O _____ star of won - der, star of night,

star with roy - al beau - ty bright,

west - ward lead - ing, still pro - ceed - ing,

guide us to thy per - fect light. light.

Additional Lyrics

4. Myrrh is mine; its bitter perfume
   Breathes a life of gathering gloom;
   Sorr'wing, sighing, bleeding, dying,
   Sealed in the stone-cold tomb.

5. Glorious now, behold Him arise,
   King and God and sacrifice.
   Alleluia, alleluia,
   Sounds through the earth and skies.

Welcome to Our World

Words and Music by Chris Rice

1. Tears are fall - ing, hearts are break - ing;
2. Hope that You don't mind our man - ger;
3. Bring Your peace in - to our vio - lence,

how we need to hear __ from God. You've been prom - ised,
how I wish we would __ have known. But long - a - wait - ed
bid our hun - gry souls __ be filled. Word now break - ing

we've been wait - ing. Wel - come, ho - ly Child,
ho - ly Stran - ger, make Your - self at home, please
Heav - en's si - lence, wel - come to our world,

1., 2.

wel - come, ho - ly Child.
make Your - self at home.
wel - come to our

3.

world. _____

What Are You Doing New Year's Eve?

By Frank Loesser

Outro-Verse

I'd ev - er be the one you chose

out of the thou - sand in - vi - ta - tions

you'll re - ceive. Ah, but in case I

stand one lit - tle chance, ___ here comes the jack - pot

ques - tion in ad - vance: ___ What are you do - ing

New Year's, New Year's Eve?

What Child Is This?

Words by William C. Dix
16th Century English Melody

First note

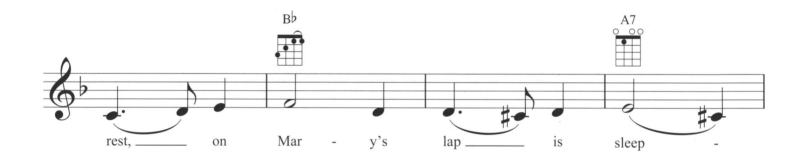

1. What Child is this, _____ who, laid to
(2., 3.) *See additional lyrics*

rest, _____ on Mar - y's lap _____ is sleep -

ing; whom an - gels greet ____ with an - thems sweet ____ while

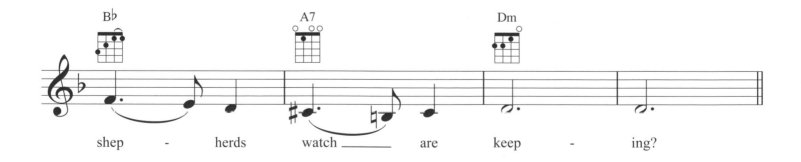

shep - herds watch _____ are keep - ing?

Chorus

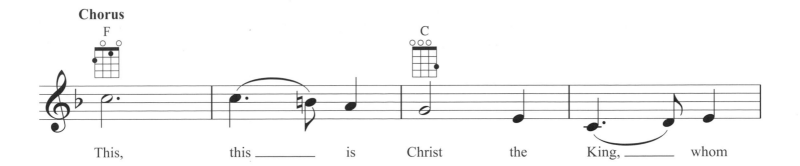

This,　　this _____ is　Christ　the　King, _____ whom

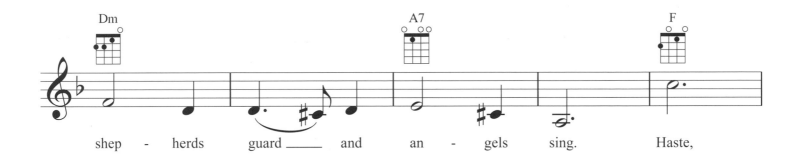

shep - herds　guard _____ and　an - gels　sing.　Haste,

haste _____ to　bring　Him　laud, _____ the　Babe, _____ the

Son _____ of　Mar - y.　2. Why　Mar - y.
　　　　　　　　　　　　　　　　　3. So

Additional Lyrics

2. Why lies He in such mean estate
   Where ox and ass are feeding?
   Good Christian, fear, for sinners here
   The silent Word is pleading.

3. So bring Him incense, gold and myrrh.
   Come, peasant, king, to own Him.
   The King of kings salvation brings;
   Let loving hearts enthrone Him.

Where's the Line to See Jesus?

Words and Music by Steve Haupt and Chris Loesch

1. Christ - mas - time was ap - proach - ing, snow was start - ing to fall, shop - pers choos - ing their pres - ents, _____ peo - ple fill - ing the mall. Chil - dren wait - ing for San - ta with ex - cite - ment and glee. A lit - tle boy _____ tugged my sweat - er, _____

𝄋 **Chorus**

looked up and asked me, "Where's the line ___ to see Je - sus? ___ Is He here at the store? If Christ - mas - time ___ is His birth - day, ___ why don't we see Him more? Where's the line ___ to see Je - sus? ___ He was born ___ for me. ___ San - ta Claus brought me pres - ents, ___ but

As the tears filled my eyes, _____ thought I heard him

sing,

Coda 1

me." In the blink of an eye, at the

Bridge

D.S. al Coda 1

sound of His trump, we'll all stand in line at His throne. Ev-'ry

knee shall bow down, ev-'ry tongue will con-fess that Je-sus Christ is

Coda 2
Outro

D.S. al Coda 2

Lord. _____

me. _____

White Christmas

from the Motion Picture Irving Berlin's HOLIDAY INN
Words and Music by Irving Berlin

First note

Chorus
Moderately slow, in 2

I'm dream - ing of a white

Christ - mas, just like the ones I used to

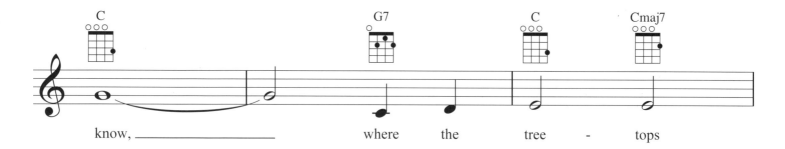

know, _____ where the tree - tops

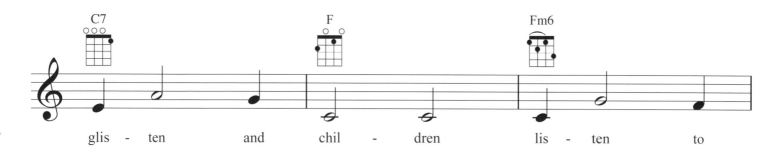

glis - ten and chil - dren lis - ten to

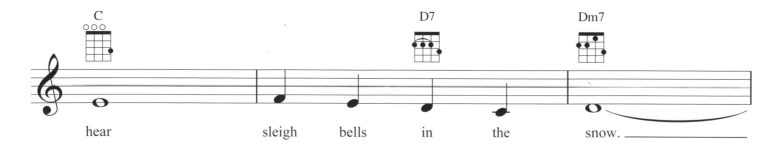

hear sleigh bells in the snow. _____

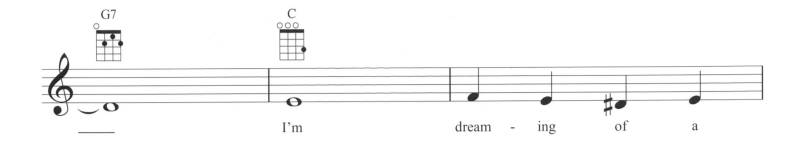

I'm dream - ing of a

white Christ - mas with ev - 'ry

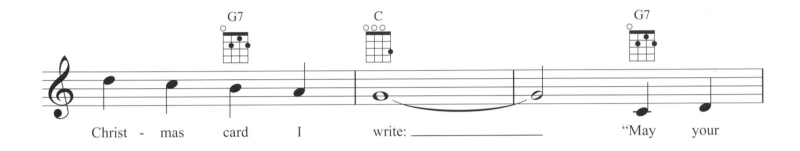

Christ - mas card I write: _____ "May your

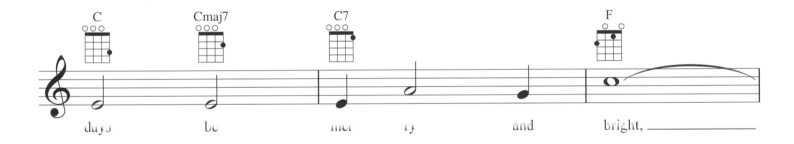

days be mer - ry and bright, _____

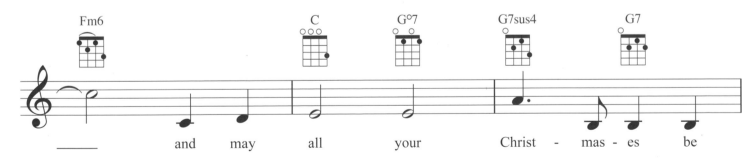

_____ and may all your Christ - mas - es be

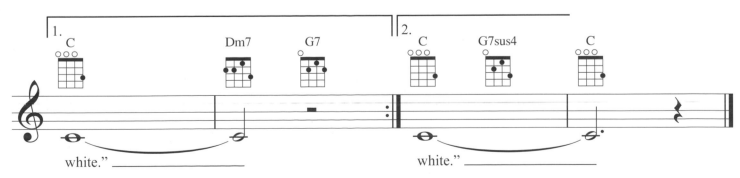

1.
white." _____

2.
white." _____

Who Would Imagine a King

from THE PREACHER'S WIFE
Words and Music by Mervyn Warren and Hallerin Hilton Hill

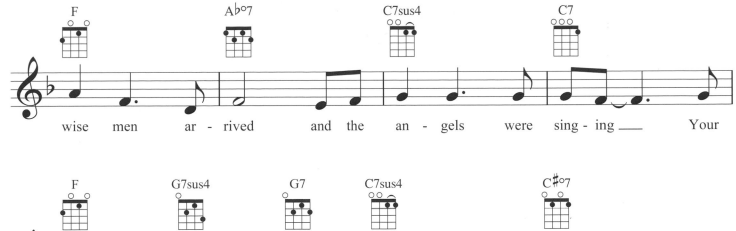

wise men ar - rived and the an - gels were sing - ing ____ Your

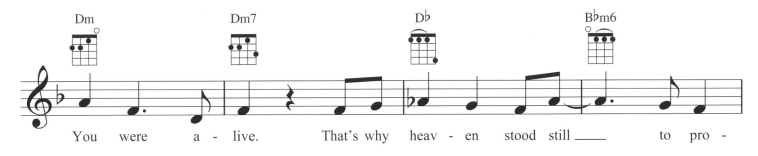

name that the world would be dif - f'rent 'cause

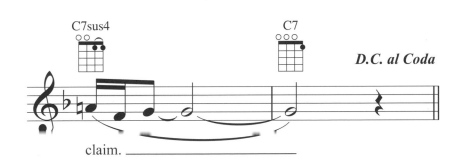

You were a - live. That's why heav - en stood still ____ to pro -

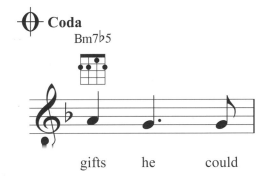

D.C. al Coda

Coda

claim. ____

gifts he could

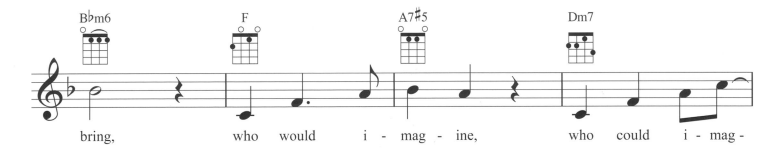

bring, who would i - mag - ine, who could i - mag -

- ine, who would i - mag - ine a King? ____

Winter Snow

Words and Music by Audrey Assad

slow; fall - ing _____ from the sky _____ in the night _____

_____ to the earth _____ be - low. _____

Verse

2. You could -'ve swept in _____ like a tid - al _____ wave, _____ or _____ in an o -

- cean _____ to rav - age _____ our _____ hearts. _____ You _____ could have come _____

_____ through _____ like a roar - ing flood _____ to wipe _____

_____ a - way _____ the things we've _____ scarred. Oh, _____ but You came _____

Chorus

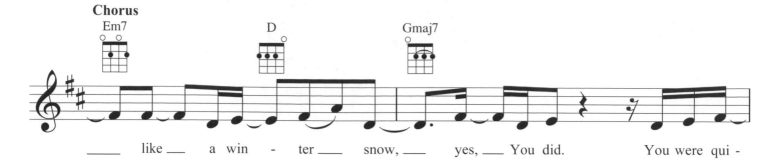

_____ like _____ a win - ter _____ snow, _____ yes, _____ You did. You were qui -

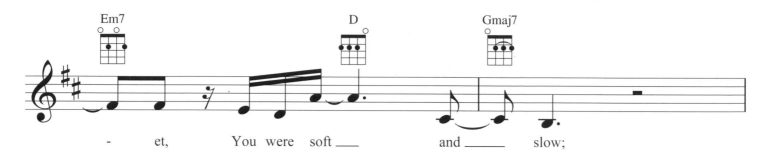

- et, You were soft _____ and _____ slow;

fall - ing _____ from the sky _____ in the night _____ to the earth be - low.

Bridge

Ooh, no, _____ Your voice _____ was - n't in _____

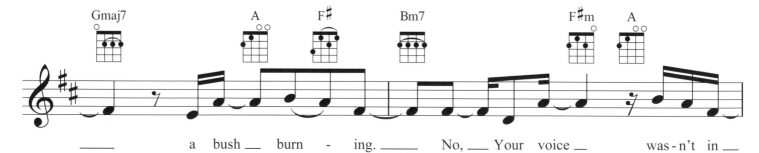

_____ a bush _____ burn - ing. _____ No, _____ Your voice _____ was - n't in _____

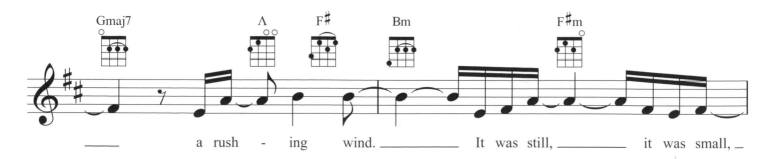

_____ a rush - ing wind. _____ It was still, _____ it was small, _____

it was hid - den.

Chorus

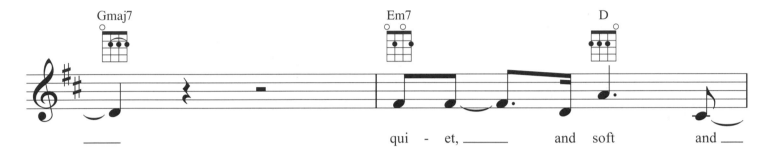

Oh, You came like a win - ter snow:

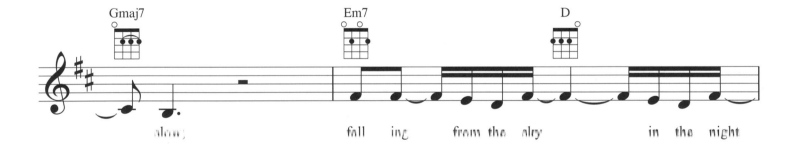

qui - et, and soft and

along fall - ing from the sky in the night

to the earth be - low. You came

Outro

fall - ing from the sky in the night to the earth be - low.

219

Winter Wonderland

Words by Dick Smith
Music by Felix Bernard

Where Are You Christmas?

from Dr. Seuss' HOW THE GRINCH STOLE CHRISTMAS

Words and Music by Will Jennings, James Horner and Mariah Carey

First note

Verse
Gently, in 2

1. Where are you, Christ - mas? Why can't I find you?
4. I feel you, Christ - mas. I know I found you.

Why have you gone a - way? _____
You nev - er fade a - way. _____

Verse

2. Where is the laugh - ter you used to bring me?
3. Where are you, Christ - mas? Do you re - mem - ber
5. The joy of Christ - mas stays here in - side us,

To Coda

Why can't I hear mu - sic play? _____
the one you used to _____ know? _____
fills each and ev - 'ry _____

_____
My world is chang - ing. _____
I'm not the same one. _____

I'm re-ar-rang-ing.   Does that mean
See what the time's done.   Is that mean why

Christ - mas   chang - es
you ___ have   let _____ me

1.
too? _____

2.   **Bridge**
go? _____   Oh. _____   Christ - mas is

here, ___   ev - 'ry - where, _____   oh. _____

Christ - mas is here ___   if you care. ___

If there is love ___ in your

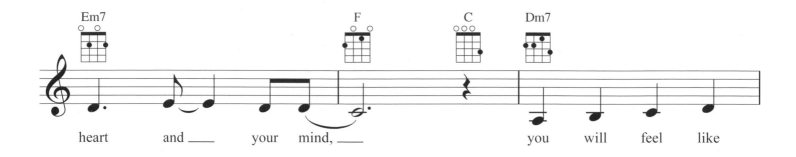

heart and ___ your mind, ___ you will feel like

D.C. al Coda

Christ - mas all the time. ___

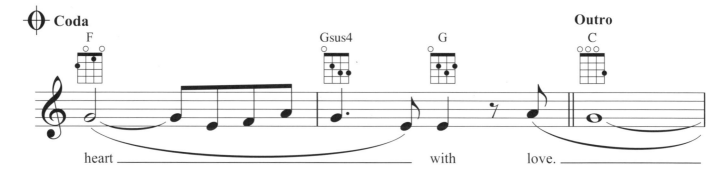

Coda

Outro

heart ___ with love. ___

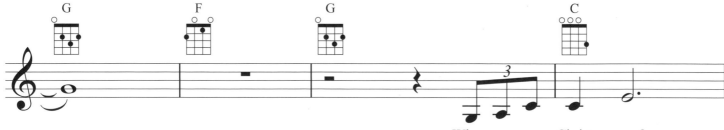

___ Where are you, Christ - mas?

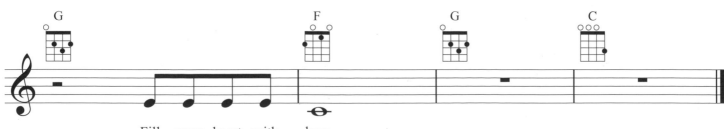

Fill your heart with love.